Somatic Exercise Made Simple

Learn Gentle, Accessible Exercises for Pain Relief, Stress Reduction, Improved Mobility, and Deep Relaxation Techniques to Enhance Your Mental and Physical Health

Dr. Danielle Griffin

Empower Press, LLC

Book Cover by Ashish S. Joshi

Photographs by Darius Wiggins of The G.A.T.E. Photography, Humble, TX

About the author

Dr. Danielle Griffin has a Doctorate of Education in organizational leadership, with an emphasis in organizational development, and spent time as a University Adjunct professor. In her business life, she coaches others to define how they want to grow personally and professionally, including continuing education, training, and development or starting and growing their businesses. Danielle has 10+ years as a yoga practitioner and is a 200-hour certified yoga instructor specializing in Vinyasa, restorative yoga, and trauma-informed somatic exercise therapy. She is also a Certified Hypnotherapist trained by the renowned Hypnotherapist and NLP practitioner Paul McKenna. Her expertise in these areas is unparalleled, and

Danielle is excited to share her new book "Somatic Exercise Made Simple." She seeks to continue to help others grow and heal holistically by publishing empowering books and sharing her knowledge and skills with others to help them lead happier and healthier lives. Danielle helps others through coaching and hosting live yoga sessions, somatic exercise sessions, and hypnotherapy sessions. She's spent over a decade exploring the mind-body connection, and her journey has been transformative. She understands this path's challenges and rewards, and her personal growth resonates with those she helps. Her passion for helping others improve their lives through mindfulness and movement has led her to create this book, a guide designed to make somatic exercises accessible and effective for everyone. She coaches other entrepreneurs and individuals with the mindset to overcome self-doubt and limiting beliefs and manifest the lives they want for themselves. She hopes to share her experience with yoga, meditation, and hypnotherapy so that it can have a positive impact on the lives of others.

Author Dr. Danielle Griffin

Acknowledgements

I want to thank my husband, Clarence, and our sons for supporting this effort and encouraging me to pursue my passion for helping others.

I want to thank the videographer, Visionary Masterminds, LLC, of Houston, TX, for your work recording the footage for the bonus videos.

I would also like to thank the photographer, Darius Wiggins of The G.A.T.E. Photography, for the photography use of your studio to capture the images for the book.

Thank you to Ashish S. Joshi for your creativity and flexibility in creating the book cover.

Bonus Videos - Supplemental Content to Support Your Goals

Congratulations! Your book comes with Bonus video content, of the author and certified instructor performing many of the poses described in this book. Much time and effort went into making these videos. As a trained instructor, Danielle guides you through proper form and modifications to achieve maximum benefits. Correct form and alignment are essential to prevent injuries and ensure you also benefit from the exercise. In addition, awareness of breath cues is vital for optimal somatic benefit.

Remember, if the move is demonstrated on one side, please be sure to alternate sides to balance the body, even if you only feel tight or discomfort on one side of your body. It's important to not only focus on one side.

The video guide, combined with the detailed step-by-step breath-to-movement instructions in the book, makes it easy to feel confident about performing the moves in this book. We make somatic exercise simple!

How to Download:

1. Click the link or scan the QR code below

2. Complete the form

3. Then, access the private link and bookmark the page. This link is only available to our readers and is not publicly available. By completing the form, you will also receive a confirmation email with the link to access the videos.

https://mailchi.mp/318cab5806fc/somatic-exercise-made-simple-videos

QR Code to Access
Bonus Video Content

Contents

Introduction

We all have moments when life feels like a relentless grind. Busy schedules, mounting stress, and the nagging pain that never entirely disappears can make even the simplest tasks seem overwhelming. Here is a story that might sound familiar.

Meet Lisa, a 35-year-old marketing executive. She's always on the go, juggling deadlines, meetings, and a family. The stress manifests as chronic back pain and tension headaches, leaving her exhausted and irritable. Traditional exercise routines and medications offer temporary relief, but nothing seems to address the root of her problems. One day, a friend introduces her to somatic exercises—a gentle, mindful approach to movement that promises relief and transformation. Skeptical but desperate, Lisa gives it a try. Within weeks, she experienced not only significant pain relief but also a profound sense of calm and well-being she hadn't felt in years. This is the hope and transformation somatic exercises can bring to your life.

I'm Dr. Danielle Griffin, and like Lisa, I've faced my battles with stress and physical discomfort. As a 200-hour certified Yoga instructor and Certified Hypnotherapist, I've spent over a decade exploring the mind-body connection. My journey with yoga and meditation has been transformative. Still, it wasn't until I discovered somatic therapy that I found a holistic approach that truly addresses both physical and mental well-being. My passion for helping others improve their lives through mindfulness and movement has led me to create this book, a guide designed to make somatic exercises accessible and effective for everyone.

So, what exactly are somatic exercises? Unlike traditional workouts focusing on external performance and muscle strength, somatic exercises emphasize mobility and the mind-body experience. They are about becoming aware of how your body feels and moves, fostering a deeper connection between your mind and body. By focusing on conscious movement and body awareness, somatic exercises help you release tension, reduce pain, and enhance overall mobility.

The purpose of this book is simple yet profound: to offer you a step-by-step guide to somatic therapy that can help you manage stress, anxiety, and chronic pain while improving your overall well-being. We've designed a holistic program tailored for busy, health-conscious adults like you who seek mind-body harmony. With daily practice, you will see a mind-body transformation within 30 days. The program includes modifications for various levels of mobility and evidence-based explanations of its benefits. Our goal is to provide an instructional and inspirational resource, guiding you through a transformative journey toward better health.

My vision for this book is to create a comprehensive, easy-to-follow program incorporating diverse somatic exercises and meditation techniques. Whether you're a beginner or someone with more experience, this book is inclusive and adaptable, catering to various physical capability levels. Emphasizing the privacy and comfort of practicing at home, it requires no special equipment, making it accessible to everyone.

What sets this book apart is its holistic approach. Our 30-day program doesn't just focus on physical exercises; it also integrates mindful meditation, breathwork practices, and evidence-based explanations of the benefits of somatic therapy. Throughout the book, you'll find personal stories and case studies that inspire and guide you, showing you that you're not alone on this journey.

Let me give you a brief overview of what to expect. We'll start by understanding the basics of somatic exercises and gradually move toward integrating these practices into a holistic lifestyle. Each chapter will provide detailed instructions, high-quality visuals, and modifications for various levels of mobility. From basic concepts to advanced practices, this book will guide you step-by-step, ensuring you feel supported and empowered throughout your journey.

This book is for adults looking for holistic methods to improve their well-being, regardless of their fitness level or familiarity with somatic practices. Whether you're new to this or have some experience, you'll find the content accessible and informative. The exercises can be performed anywhere by anyone, reinforcing our commitment to inclusivity. You are welcomed and considered in this journey to better health.

We've also taken great care to ensure that the information provided is credible and reliable by drawing on scientific research, clinical studies, and statistics. This book offers an evidence-based approach to somatic exercises. You can trust that the practices recommended here are practical and grounded in solid research. This reassurance should give you confidence in the effectiveness of somatic exercises.

As you read this book, I encourage you to approach it with an open mind and a commitment to your well-being. The journey you're about to embark on holds the potential to transform your life in ways you might not have imagined. This book isn't just a guide; it's a companion on your path to balance, wellness, and a deeper connection with your body.

On a personal note, I want to share how somatic exercises have transformed my approach to health and wellness. Like many of you, I've struggled with stress and physical discomfort. Discovering somatic therapy was a turning point that deepened my connection to my body and brought me a sense of peace and well-being that I hadn't experienced before. I'm excited to share this journey with you and to support you every step of the way.

Let's begin this transformative journey together. With compassion, mindfulness, and a commitment to self-care, we can achieve balance, wellness, and a deeper connection with our bodies. Welcome to your path to mind-body harmony.

Chapter 1: Foundations of Somatic Exercises

A few years ago, I met John, a 45-year-old software engineer who was struggling with chronic shoulder pain and debilitating stress. Despite trying various forms of physical therapy, medication, and even meditation, nothing seemed to provide lasting relief. His work demanded long hours hunched over a computer, contributing to his discomfort. When I introduced John to somatic exercises, he was skeptical but willing to try them. Within a few weeks, he noticed a significant reduction in his shoulder pain and a newfound sense of calm that permeated his daily life. John's story is a testament to the transformative power of somatic practices, and it's just one example of how these exercises can profoundly impact your well-being.

1.1 What is Somatic Exercise? Understanding the Basics

The term' somatic' comes from the Greek word "soma," meaning body. Coined by Thomas Hanna, a pioneer in the field, somatic exercises refer to a form of movement therapy that emphasizes the internal experience of movement and body awareness. Hanna developed these exercises in the 1970s, building on Feldenkrais and Alexander Technique principles. Unlike traditional exercises focusing on external performance and muscle strength, somatic exercises are all about reconnecting with your body, understanding its signals, and moving mindfully. These exercises aim to re-educate your movement patterns, allowing you to release chronic tension and move more freely.

The core of somatic exercises are principles that set them apart from other physical activities. Mindfulness is paramount—performing each movement with full attention to the sensations it generates within the body. This heightened awareness helps you identify and consciously release areas of chronic tension. Body awareness is another fundamental principle that encourages you to understand how your body moves and feels deeply. Finally, these exercises aim to re-educate your neuromuscular system, correcting maladaptive movement patterns developed over years of stress or injury.

Consider how somatic exercises differ from yoga or traditional strength training. Yoga often emphasizes flexibility and strength through postures and strength training is used for maintaining or growing muscle and endurance. Somatic exercises concentrate on the neuromuscular system and conscious movement. The goal is not to achieve a particular pose or lift a certain weight but to experience and improve how your body moves. This focus on internal sensation rather than external achievement makes somatic exercises uniquely effective in addressing chronic pain, stress, and other conditions tied to habitual muscle tension.

The benefits of somatic exercises are extensive and varied, making them valuable to any wellness routine. One of the most immediate benefits is increased flexibility. By consciously releasing tension, your muscles can move more freely, enhancing your range of motion. Reduced pain is another significant advantage. Many people, like John, find that these exercises alleviate chronic discomfort by addressing its root causes rather than just the symptoms. You will likely experience improved posture, as re-educating your movement patterns helps you stand, sit, and move with alignment and ease. These benefits are achieved through mindful, deliberate practice, making somatic exercises a powerful tool for anyone seeking to improve their physical and mental well-being.

Integrating somatic exercises into your daily life can help you experience these benefits firsthand. This book will guide you through various exercises designed to be accessible and effective, regardless of your current fitness level or familiarity with the practice. You'll discover a path to a healthier, more balanced life through mindful movement and body awareness.

1.2 The Science of Stress and How Somatic Exercises Help

Stress is inevitable in modern life, but its impact on our bodies can be profound. When we face chronic stress, our nervous system remains constantly alert, often leading to numerous physical symptoms. The sympathetic nervous system, responsible for the "fight or flight" response, kicks into high gear, causing an increase in heart rate and muscle tension and releasing stress hormones like cortisol. Over time, this constant state of readiness can lead to muscle fatigue, headaches, digestive issues, and a general sense of exhaustion. It's like driving a car with the accelerator pressed down—eventually, something is bound to break down.

Somatic exercises offer a unique way to address this by directly interacting with the nervous system. These exercises help activate the parasympathetic nervous system—the "rest and digest" counterpart to the sympathetic system when you focus on slow, mindful movements. This shift promotes relaxation and allows the body to release built-up tension. Imagine slowly easing your foot off the car's accelerator, allowing the engine to cool down and the vehicle to run more smoothly. Somatic exercises work similarly by encouraging the body to move from a constant state of alertness to calm and relaxation.

A fascinating aspect of somatic exercises is their ability to promote neuroplasticity—the brain's ability to reorganize itself by forming new neural connections. Neuroplasticity plays a crucial role in learning new skills, recovering from injuries, and improving mental health. When you engage in somatic exercises, you're not just moving your muscles but also retraining your brain to recognize and adopt healthier movement patterns. Engaging in somatic exercise can improve mental and physical health, helping you break free from the cycle of stress and tension.

Research supports the benefits of somatic exercises in managing stress and enhancing well-being. A study published in the Journal of Bodywork and Movement Therapies found that participants who practiced somatic exercises reported significantly reduced stress and improved mood compared to a control group. Another study in the Clinical Journal of Pain highlighted the effectiveness of somatic exercises in reducing chronic pain and improving overall quality of life. These findings underscore the power of mindful movement in fostering health and resilience.

Incorporating somatic exercises into your routine can be a game-changer. Focusing on the internal experience of movement makes you more attuned to your body's signals, allowing you to respond to stress in healthier ways. Whether it's a simple neck roll to release tension or a series of gentle stretches to improve flexibility, these exercises offer a practical and effective means of managing stress and enhancing your overall well-being.

So, as you begin to explore somatic exercises, remember that you're not just moving your body—you're also nurturing your mind. This holistic approach can help you achieve balance and harmony, making it easier to navigate the challenges of daily life with grace and resilience.

1.3 Exploring the Mind-Body Connection in Somatic Theory

The mind-body connection has intrigued philosophers and healers for centuries. In somatic theory, this connection is foundational. Drawing from Eastern philosophies like Taoism and Ayurveda, which emphasize harmony between mind and body, somatic exercises integrate these age-old principles with modern psychological theories. The idea is simple yet profound: our mental states and physical conditions are deeply interconnected. When we engage in somatic practices, we are not merely moving our bodies but also nurturing our minds.

Somatic exercises employ both biomechanics and psychological awareness to foster this connection. Biomechanics refers to the study of the mechanical laws relating to the movement or structure of living organisms. When you perform a somatic exercise, you're not just stretching a muscle or rotating a joint but also paying close attention to the sensations these movements produce. This heightened awareness allows you to identify and release tension, improving both physical function and emotional well-being. It's similar to how a dancer feels every muscle and joint in their body while performing, fully engaged in the experience.

The concept of interconnectedness within somatic theory highlights the constant communication between the mind and body. Stress, for example, often manifests as muscle tension. When you're anxious, your shoulders might hunch, or your jaw could clench. Conversely, your body posture can significantly impact your mood. Standing tall with an open chest can make you feel more confident and relaxed. This bidirectional relationship means that improving your physical state through somatic exercises can also enhance your mental state, creating a positive feedback loop.

Various cultures and medical traditions have historically recognized the mind-body connection. Traditional Chinese Medicine (TCM), for instance, incorporates practices like Tai Chi and acupuncture, designed to balance the body's energy and improve overall health. Ayurveda, an ancient Indian system of medicine, also emphasizes the harmony between mind and body, prescribing yoga and meditation as part of its holistic approach to health. These traditions have long understood what modern science is beginning to validate: our physical and mental health are inextricably linked.

Awareness is the cornerstone of somatic practice. Before you can address any issue, you must first become aware of it. Mindfulness—paying attention to the present moment without judgment—is the first step in somatic exercises. By tuning into your body's sensations, you can better understand its needs and respond appropriately. This practice of mindful awareness helps you break the cycle of stress and tension, leading to a more balanced and harmonious life.

Consider the story of Mary, a 50-year-old teacher with chronic neck pain. Traditional treatments provided little relief. When she started practicing somatic exercises, she began by simply becoming aware of her body. She noticed how stress made her shoulders tense and how she often held her breath when anxious. Through mindful movement and focused breathing, Mary learned to release this tension, leading to significant pain reduction and an improved sense of well-being.

To cultivate mind-body awareness, start with simple somatic exercises. Begin your day with a body scan—lying down or sitting comfortably, close your eyes, and mentally scan your body from head to toe, noting any areas of tension. Another practical exercise is mindful walking. As you walk, pay attention to each step, the sensation of your feet touching the ground, and the rhythm of your breath. These small practices can make a big difference in how connected you feel to your body, setting the stage for more profound somatic work.

1.4 The Role of the Vagus Nerve in Somatic Relaxation

The vagus nerve is one of our nervous system's most vital yet often overlooked components. Stretching from the brainstem down to the abdomen, it plays a crucial role in regulating the parasympathetic nervous system, which governs our body's restoration responses. Imagine it as a kind of internal communication highway, sending signals that help control functions like heart rate, digestion, and even mood. When stimulated correctly, the vagus nerve can facilitate deep relaxation, promoting healing and reducing stress. In a world where stress is a constant companion, understanding and leveraging the power of the vagus nerve can be transformative.

Somatic exercises offer a unique way to stimulate the vagus nerve, enhancing relaxation and emotional calm. By focusing on mindful, deliberate movements, these exercises help activate this crucial nerve, encouraging the body to shift from a state of tension to one of relaxation. Picture gently stretching your neck or engaging in deep diaphragmatic breathing—these actions send calming signals through the vagus nerve, telling your body it's safe to relax. This process alleviates physical tension and fosters emotional well-being, making it easier to navigate life's challenges with a sense of calm and balance.

Specific techniques are effective vagus nerve activators because they are simple and effective. Deep **diaphragmatic breathing**, for example, is a powerful method. By breathing deeply and slowly, you engage the diaphragm fully, stimulating the vagus nerve and promoting relaxation.

Try It Yourself: Diaphragmatic Breathing

1. Sit or lie comfortably; place one or both hands on your abdomen.

2. Inhale deeply through your nose, allowing your stomach to rise.

3. Exhale slowly through your mouth, feeling your stomach fall.

4. Repeat this for several minutes to experience a noticeable shift in your state of mind. Feel the rise and fall of your abdomen with your hands.

Diaphragmatic Breathing while Laying Down

Gentle neck stretches also work wonders.

Try It Yourself: Gentle Neck Stretches

1. Take a seated or standing position. Exhale and slowly tilt the top of your head to the left side. Feel the stretch through the right side of your neck.

2. Holding the stretch for a few breaths, Inhale and raise your head back to the center. Then, repeat on the other side.

3. Option to apply gentle pressure to your head with your opposite hand to deepen the stretch or press your right hand down towards the ground when you tilt your head to the left.

4. These simple actions can have profound effects, helping to release tension and enhance your overall sense

of calm.

Neck Stretch

Improving vagal tone—measuring how well the vagus nerve functions—offers numerous health benefits. Enhanced vagal tone can lead to better digestion, as the vagus nerve is crucial in regulating digestive processes. Imagine enjoying meals without the discomfort of indigestion or bloating simply because your body is more relaxed. Improved vagal tone also reduces heart rate, promoting cardiovascular health and reducing the risk of heart-related issues. Additionally, a well-functioning vagus nerve can elevate your mood by influencing the production of neurotransmitters like serotonin and dopamine, which are vital for emotional well-being. Regular practice of somatic exercises helps you feel better physically and supports mental health, leading to a more balanced and fulfilling life.

Understanding the vagus nerve's role in somatic relaxation opens possibilities for improving your health and well-being. By incorporating simple, mindful practices into your daily routine, you can harness the power of this remarkable nerve to foster relaxation, emotional calm, and overall health.

1.5 Setting Up Your Somatic Exercise Space at Home

Creating the right environment for your somatic exercises is crucial in ensuring you get the most out of your practice. Your space should be quiet, comfortable, and free from distractions. Choose a room or a corner in your home where you can move freely without interruptions, such as your living room, bedroom, or even a dedicated exercise room if you have the luxury. The key is to find a spot where you feel at ease and can focus entirely on your movements and sensations. Inform family members or housemates of your exercise time to minimize disruptions.

The beauty of somatic exercises lies in their simplicity and accessibility. You don't need a lot of fancy gear to get started if any at all. A good-quality yoga mat is often all you need, providing a comfortable surface that supports your joints and prevents slipping. Any soft, non-slippery floor space will work if a yoga mat is unavailable. Comfortable clothing that allows for free movement is also essential, enabling you to perform exercises without restriction. Optional items like a cushion or a small pillow can be handy for specific exercises, offering additional support when needed.

Enhancing the atmosphere of your exercise space can significantly improve your experience. Soft, ambient lighting creates a calming environment that helps you focus on your practice. Consider using a dimmable lamp or even candles to set a tranquil mood. Soothing music can also be beneficial, providing a gentle background that aids relaxation and concentration. Choose instrumental tracks or nature sounds that won't distract you from your movements. Aromatherapy is another beautiful addition—diffuse essential oils like lavender or eucalyptus to promote a sense of calm and well-being. The goal is to create a sanctuary where you can escape the stresses of daily life and connect deeply with your body.

Ensuring safety during your somatic exercises is paramount. Start by checking the flooring of your chosen space. It should be even and stable, without any loose rugs or clutter that could cause you to trip or slip. If you're using a yoga mat, ensure it's laid flat and securely on the floor. As you begin your exercises, move slowly and mindfully, paying attention to how your body feels. Avoid pushing yourself into any movement that causes pain or discomfort. Remember, somatic exercises are about gentle, conscious movement, not forceful stretching or intense exertion. It's essential to listen to your body and respect its limits.

Common mistakes include holding your breath, rushing through movements, or ignoring pain signals. Holding your breath can increase tension, so remind yourself to breathe deeply and steadily throughout your practice. Rushing can lead to improper form and an increased risk of injury, so take your time with each movement, focusing on the quality rather than the speed. Finally, if you experience pain, stop the exercise immediately and reassess. Pain is your body's way of telling you something isn't right, so heed its warnings and adjust as necessary. Setting up a safe and inviting space lays the groundwork for a fulfilling and effective somatic practice.

1.6 Essential Somatic Movements: An Overview

Let's begin with some foundational somatic movements that are particularly effective for beginners. One such movement is the **Cat-Cow stretch**. This exercise is performed on all fours and involves alternating between arching your back toward the ceiling (Cat) and dropping your belly towards the floor while lifting your head (Cow).

Try It Yourself: Cat-Cow Stretch

1. Start on your hands and knees with your wrists directly under your shoulders and your knees under your hips in a tabletop position.

2. Inhale, and move into the Cow position by raising your gaze towards the ceiling, arching your back while dropping your belly towards the ground, and lifting your tailbone towards the ceiling.

3. On the exhale, transition into the Cat position by tucking your chin to your chest, drawing your navel towards your spine, and tucking your pelvis. Repeat this flow for several breaths, moving slowly and mindfully.

4. **Modification:** If kneeling is uncomfortable, perform the pose in a seated position on a chair. Place your hands on your knees, and as you inhale, arch your back and lift your chest. On the exhale, round your spine and tuck your chin.

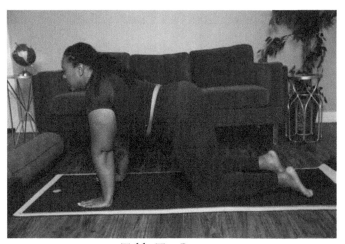

Table Top Position

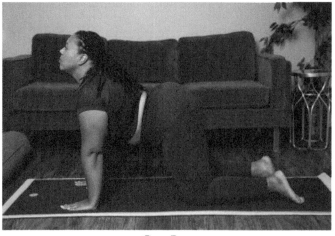

Cow Pose

Cat Pose

Another foundational movement is the **Pelvic Tilt**. Perform this exercise while lying on your back with your knees bent and feet flat on the floor.

Try It Yourself: Pelvic Tilt

1. Begin by placing your hands on your hips to feel the movement. Inhale, tilt your pelvis forward, and arch your lower back slightly off the floor.

2. Exhale and tilt your pelvis backward, pressing your lower back gently into the floor. This simple motion helps to release tension in the lower back and improve pelvic mobility. Perform this movement slowly, paying close attention to how your lower back and pelvis feel with each tilt.

3. **Modification:** If lying on the floor is challenging, try performing the movement while seated on a chair. Sit towards the edge of the chair with your feet flat on the floor and your hands on your hips, then tilt your pelvis forward and backward in the same manner.

Each of these movements offers specific benefits that align with the principles of somatic exercises. The Cat-Cow stretch, for example, increases spinal flexibility and helps release back and neck tension, promoting better posture and reducing chronic pain. The Pelvic Tilt, on the other hand, targets the lower back and pelvic region, areas often affected by prolonged sitting or poor posture. Daily practice of these movements can enhance your overall flexibility, reduce muscle tension, and improve your body's alignment.

Synchronizing your breath with each movement enhances the effectiveness and meditative quality of somatic exercises. Inhale deeply through your nose as you move into the initial position, and exhale slowly through your mouth as you transition. This mindful breathing supports relaxation and helps you stay present and focused on the sensations within your body. For example, while performing the Cat-Cow stretch, inhale as you move into the Cow position, feeling the expansion in your chest and abdomen. Exhale as you transition into the Cat position, noticing the gentle release of tension in your back.

Integrating these somatic exercises into your daily routine doesn't have to be complicated. Start by dedicating just a few minutes each day, perhaps in the morning, to wake up your body or in the evening to unwind. Consistency is key, so find a time that works best for you and make it a part of your daily habits. Consider setting reminders or pairing these exercises with another activity, like brushing your teeth or preparing for bed, to help establish a routine.

By incorporating these simple, foundational movements into your life, you'll experience somatic exercises' transformative benefits. Improved flexibility, reduced pain, and a deeper connection to your body are just the beginning. As you continue to practice, you'll find that these exercises enhance your physical well-being and contribute to a greater sense of mental and emotional balance. Let's move forward with this practice, embracing the positive changes it can bring to our lives.

Chapter 2: Starting Simple – Basic Techniques

Imagine waking up each morning feeling refreshed, calm, and ready to face the day, no matter the challenges. For many of us, the reality is quite different. We often wake up feeling groggy, stressed, and already behind schedule. I remember working with Mark, a 40-year-old Accountant who came to me seeking relief from chronic stress and sleep issues. His demanding job left him feeling perpetually exhausted and irritable. After incorporating some basic breathwork techniques into his daily routine, Mark experienced a dramatic improvement in his energy levels and overall sense of well-being. This chapter introduces you to the transformative power of breathwork, a cornerstone of somatic exercises.

2.1 Breathwork Basics for Relaxation and Energy Flow

Breathwork is a powerful tool that can significantly enhance physical and mental well-being. One of the simplest yet most effective techniques is **diaphragmatic breathing**. This method involves deep, intentional breaths that engage the diaphragm, the primary muscle used in respiration.

Try It Yourself: Diaphragmatic Breathing Exercise

1. Sit or lie down in a comfortable position.

2. Place one hand on your chest and the other on your abdomen.

3. Inhale deeply through your nose, expand your diaphragm, and allow your abdomen to rise while keeping your chest relatively still.

4. Exhale slowly through your mouth, feeling your abdomen fall. Repeat 5-10 times, focusing on the rise and fall of your abdomen. This technique promotes relaxation and increases oxygen intake, providing a natural energy boost.

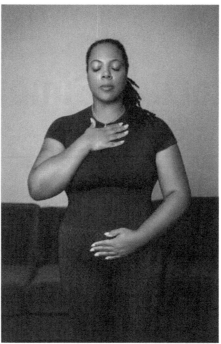

*Diaphragmatic Breathing while
standing*

Another effective breathwork technique is the **4-7-8 Breathing Method**, which is particularly useful for calming the mind and preparing for sleep.

Try It Yourself: 4-7-8 Breathing

1. Begin by sitting or lying down in a comfortable position.

2. Inhale quietly through your nose for a count of four.

3. Hold your breath for a count of seven.

4. Finally, exhale completely through your mouth, making a whooshing sound for a count of eight. Repeat this cycle three more times. The 4-7-8 technique helps regulate your breath, slow your heart rate, and reduce anxiety, making it an excellent stress management tool.

Incorporating breathwork into your daily routine can significantly enhance your somatic practice. Conscious breathing bridges your mind and body, enhancing bodily awareness and making somatic exercises more effective. When you focus on your breath, you become more attuned to the sensations in your body, allowing you to identify and release tension more easily. This heightened awareness is particularly beneficial when performing somatic exercises, enabling you to move more mindfully and efficiently.

One of the best aspects of breathwork is its versatility. You can practice these techniques almost anywhere—during your morning commute, waiting for a meeting, or watching TV. For instance, practicing diaphragmatic breathing during a stressful commute can help you arrive at your destination feeling more relaxed and focused. Similarly, the 4-7-8 technique before a meeting can help reduce anxiety and improve concentration. The key is to integrate these practices into your daily routine, making them a natural part of your life.

The physiological impact of breathwork on the nervous system is profound. Conscious breathing activates the parasympathetic nervous system, which helps to counteract the stress response triggered by the sympathetic nervous system. This activation leads to a reduction in cortisol levels, the hormone responsible for stress. Lower cortisol levels result in decreased heart rate and blood pressure, promoting a state of calm and relaxation. Additionally, increased oxygen intake from deep breathing enhances brain function and energy levels, making you more alert and focused.

Breathwork offers a practical and effective solution for reducing stress, enhancing energy, or feeling more connected to your body. Just like Mark, you, too, can transform your daily life by making these techniques a regular part of your routine and improving your physical and mental well-being.

2.2 Gentle Neck and Shoulder Releases for Desk Workers

When you spend hours hunched over a desk, it's no wonder your neck and shoulders feel like concrete. The tension builds gradually, often unnoticed, until it becomes persistent stiffness and pain. But there's hope. The exercises we're about to introduce can bring you relief and comfort, making your workday more bearable. Those who work in front of a computer, where the spine's natural curve gets compromised, often suffer from this pain, leading to muscle imbalances. The repetitive strain of typing and the forward head posture place immense stress on the cervical spine and shoulder muscles. The result? Chronic discomfort can affect everything from your concentration to your overall mood.

The **neck roll** is one of the simplest yet most effective exercises to release neck tension. It's a straightforward movement you can do anytime, anywhere, empowering you to take control of your comfort and well-being.

Try It Yourself: Neck Roll Exercise

1. Sit comfortably in your chair with your feet flat on the ground.

2. Slowly drop your chin to your chest, feeling the stretch along the back of your neck.

3. Gently roll your head towards your right shoulder, tilt it back slightly, and finally roll it towards your left shoulder before returning to the starting position.

4. Repeat this movement several times, moving slowly and mindfully. This exercise helps to stretch the neck muscles, improving flexibility and reducing tension.

Neck Roll Position 1

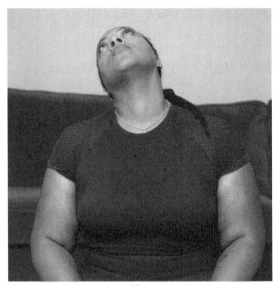

Neck Roll Position 2

Neck Roll

Another beneficial exercise is the **shoulder shrug**.

Try It Yourself: Shoulder Shrug Exercise

1. Sit or stand with your arms relaxed by your sides.

2. Inhale as you lift your shoulders towards your ears, squeezing them tightly.

3. Hold for a few seconds, then exhale as you release your shoulders to their natural position.

4. Repeat this movement for about 10 repetitions. The shoulder shrug targets the trapezius muscles, which, if you're a desk worker, are often tight and overworked. Regularly practicing this exercise can alleviate tension and improve shoulder mobility.

Shoulder Shrug

Consider taking short breaks every hour to perform these exercises. For example, stand up and do a few shoulder shrugs during a quick break between meetings. Or, if you're waiting for a file to download, take a moment to do some neck rolls. These minor interruptions help release physical tension and give your mind a much-needed break, improving overall productivity and focus.

The long-term benefits of regularly practicing these exercises are significant. Over time, you'll notice a reduction in chronic pain and an improvement in your posture. Consistent practice helps to re-educate your muscles, teaching them to maintain a more relaxed state even during stressful periods. Improved alignment of the neck and shoulders can also enhance your breathing by allowing your chest to expand more fully, promoting better oxygen flow, which can boost your energy levels and mental clarity. So, stay committed to these exercises, and you'll see the difference they can make in your life.

Additionally, these exercises can prevent the development of more severe conditions such as cervical spondylosis or tension headaches. You're treating the symptoms and preventing future issues by addressing the root cause of muscle stiffness and imbalance. It's like giving your neck and shoulders a daily tune-up, ensuring they remain flexible and pain-free.

Imagine the relief of finishing your workday without the usual aches and pains, feeling more relaxed and alert. Integrating these simple exercises into your routine can make a world of difference. Whether at your desk or taking a short break, these movements are easy to perform and incredibly effective. So, next time you feel that familiar tension creeping in, take a few minutes to practice these gentle releases and experience the benefits for yourself.

2.3 Somatic Exercises to Ease Lower Back Pain

Lower back pain is a common issue that plagues many adults, often due to poor posture, prolonged sitting, or stress. The lower back, or lumbar region, supports much of the body's weight, making it particularly susceptible to strain and discomfort. For instance, sitting without proper lumbar support can lead to muscle imbalances and tightness. Lifting heavy objects incorrectly or even emotional stress can also cause the muscles in the lower back to tense up, contributing to chronic pain. Somatic exercises provide a holistic approach to alleviating discomfort by targeting the root causes of tension and imbalance.

The **pelvic tilt is an** effective somatic movement for lower back pain.

Try It Yourself: Pelvic Tilt Exercise

1. Begin by lying on your back with your knees bent and feet flat on the floor.

2. Place your hands on your hips to feel the movement.

3. Inhale deeply, then exhale as you tilt your pelvis backward, gently pressing your lower back into the floor.

4. Inhale again as you return to a neutral position.

5. Repeat this movement several times, focusing on sensations in your lower back and pelvis. This exercise

helps release tension in the lumbar region and strengthen the spine's muscles.

Pelvic Tilt

The **knee-to-chest** stretch is another effective somatic movement for lower back pain.

Try It Yourself: Knee-to-Chest Stretch

1. While still lying on your back, bring one knee towards your chest, holding it with both hands. Keep the other leg bent with the foot flat on the floor.

2. Inhale deeply, then exhale as you gently pull your knee closer to your chest.

3. Hold this position for a few breaths, then switch legs.

4. This stretch targets the lower back and glutes, helping to alleviate tension and improve flexibility. Regularly performing this exercise can significantly reduce lower back discomfort and enhance range of motion.

Knee to Chest Stretch

Integrating these exercises into your daily routine is key to maintaining a healthy back. For instance,

1. Start your morning with a few pelvic tilts to strengthen your lower back muscles.

2. During the day, especially if you have a desk job, take short breaks to do the knee-to-chest stretch.

Daily preventative measures are essential for avoiding the recurrence of lower back pain. In addition to the exercises, one of the most effective strategies is maintaining proper posture while sitting and standing. Ensure that your chair provides adequate lumbar support and that your feet are flat on the floor when sitting. When lifting objects, always bend at the knees and keep the object close to your body to avoid straining your back. Regularly practicing somatic exercises helps to reinforce these good habits, making them second nature over time.

Another preventative measure is staying active. While avoiding movement when experiencing back pain might be tempting, gentle exercises like walking or swimming can promote healing and prevent further discomfort. These activities increase blood flow to the muscles, helping to reduce stiffness and improve flexibility. Additionally, incorporating a variety of movements into your routine ensures that all muscle groups are engaged and balanced, reducing the risk of overuse injuries.

Stress management also plays a crucial role in preventing lower back pain. Chronic stress leads to muscle tension, particularly in the back and shoulders. Practices such as mindfulness, meditation, and somatic exercises can help reduce stress levels and prevent the physical manifestations of stress. By addressing the physical and emotional aspects of lower back pain, you create a comprehensive approach to maintaining a healthy, pain-free back.

2.4 Improving Joint Health Through Somatic Movements

Joint health is a cornerstone of overall mobility and quality of life. Our joints act as the hinges and pivots that allow us to move easily and gracefully. Whether reaching for a jar on the top shelf, bending down to tie your shoes, or simply walking, healthy joints make these movements possible without pain or restriction. Unfortunately, factors like aging, repetitive strain, and sedentary lifestyles can lead to joint stiffness, discomfort, and even chronic conditions like arthritis. Somatic exercises offer a gentle yet effective way to maintain and enhance joint health by focusing on flexibility, strength, and fluid movement.

One key benefit of somatic exercises is their ability to target major joints, including the knees, elbows, and wrists. For example, the **seated knee lift** is a simple exercise for knee health.

Try It Yourself: Seated Knee Lift Exercise

1. Sit on a chair with your feet flat on the ground.

2. Slowly lift one knee towards your chest, holding it with both hands if needed for support.

3. Hold for a few seconds, then gently lower it back down.

4. Repeat this movement several times on each side. This exercise helps increase flexibility and strength in the knee joint, promoting better mobility and reducing the risk of injury. It can be performed sitting or standing.

Seated Knee Lift

Another effective exercise for the elbows is **elbow flexion and extension**.

Try It Yourself: Elbow Flexion and Extension

1. Stand or sit with your arms relaxed by your sides.

2. Slowly bend one elbow, bringing your hand towards your shoulder.

3. Hold briefly, then extend your arm back to the starting position.

4. Repeat this movement several times on each side. This exercise targets the muscles around the elbow joint, enhancing their strength and flexibility. It is particularly beneficial for tasks involving repetitive arm movements.

Elbow Extension

Elbow Flexion

For the wrists, a helpful exercise is the **wrist circles**.

Try It Yourself: Wrist Circle Exercise

1. Extend one arm in front of you with your hands in a fist.

2. Slowly rotate your wrist in a circular motion, clockwise and counterclockwise.

3. Repeat this movement several times on each side. Wrist circles help to improve the flexibility and range of motion in the wrist joint, making it easier to perform daily activities like typing or lifting objects.

4. **Modification**: Use your other hand to support the extended arm below the wrist. Make smaller, slower rotations if wrist pain or stiffness exists. The key is to listen to your body and adjust the movements to suit your comfort level.

Neutral Wrist Position

Wrist Circles

A core principle of somatic exercises is the emphasis on gentle movements. Unlike high-impact exercises that can strain the joints, somatic movements are smooth and controlled, reducing the risk of injury. This fluidity is crucial for maintaining and enhancing joint function, as it encourages the synovial fluid within the joints to flow more freely. Synovial fluid acts as a lubricant, reducing friction between the cartilage and bones and allowing for smoother, pain-free movement. Imagine it as oiling the hinges of a door to ensure it opens and closes quickly without creaking.

Regular practice of these gentle, fluid movements can significantly improve joint health. Over time, you'll notice increased flexibility, reduced pain, and improved range of motion. These benefits extend beyond physical health, contributing to a sense of ease and confidence in your daily activities. Whether gardening, playing with your grandchildren, or simply enjoying a walk in the park, healthy joints allow you to move through life with greater freedom and joy.

Chapter 3: Tailoring Somatic Practices to Your Life

Picture this: You're having a hectic workday, juggling back-to-back meetings and an overflowing email inbox. The stress is palpable, and your body feels the brunt of it—tight shoulders, a stiff neck, and that familiar ache in your lower back. Many of us know this scenario all too well. This chapter will help you find those precious moments within your busy day to incorporate somatic exercises, turning those brief breaks into powerful opportunities for stress relief and physical rejuvenation.

3.1 Somatic Exercises for the Busy Professional

Identifying opportunities for somatic breaks during your workday is crucial. It's not about adding more to your plate but about making the most of the moments you already have. Start by looking for natural pauses in your schedule, such as the few minutes before a meeting begins or the brief lull during your lunch break. Often overlooked moments throughout the day can be transformed into valuable opportunities for short somatic exercises. For instance, while waiting for a video call to start, you can do a quick seated spinal twist to release tension in your back and shoulders. By identifying and utilizing these small windows of time, you can seamlessly integrate somatic practices into your daily routine without feeling overwhelmed.

Desk-based movements are particularly effective for busy professionals. One simple yet powerful exercise is the **seated spinal twist**.

Try It Yourself: Seated Spinal Twist

1. Sit up straight in your chair with your feet flat on the floor.

2. Place your right hand on the back of the chair and your left hand on your right knee. Inhale deeply, then exhale as you gently twist your torso to the right, looking over your right shoulder.

3. Hold for a few breaths, then repeat on the other side. This twist helps to relieve tension in the spine and improves overall flexibility.

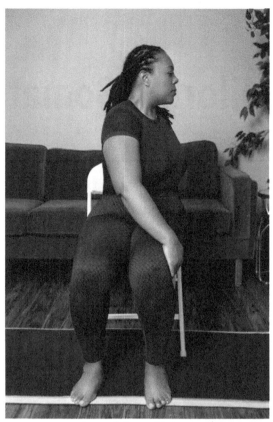

Seated Spinal Twist

Another effective desk-based movement is the **shoulder shrug**.

Try It Yourself: Shoulder Shrug Exercise

1. Sit or stand with your arms relaxed by your sides.

2. Inhale deeply as you lift your shoulders towards your ears, squeezing them tightly.

3. Hold for a few seconds, then exhale as you release your shoulders.

4. Repeat this movement for about 10 repetitions. The shoulder shrug targets the trapezius muscles, which desk workers often feel are tight and overworked. It helps alleviate tension and improve focus.

Shoulder Shrug

One practical approach to creating a daily routine is to set reminders on your phone or computer to prompt you to take short somatic breaks throughout the day. These reminders can be as simple as a gentle chime or a pop-up notification encouraging stretching and breathing. Another strategy is to link somatic exercises to existing habits. For example, whenever you sip water or finish a meeting, take a moment to perform a quick somatic exercise. By associating these practices with routine activities, you create a seamless integration that becomes second nature over time.

Stress management is another critical aspect of somatic exercises, especially in high-pressure environments. Techniques specifically targeting stress relief can help professionals manage stress in real-time. One effective method is the **4-7-8 breathing technique**. Stress management is another critical aspect of somatic exercises, especially in high-pressure environments. Techniques specifically targeting stress relief can help professionals manage stress in real-time. One effective method is the 4-7-8 breathing technique. It's simple, it's quick, and it's remarkably effective.

Try It Yourself: 4-7-8 Breathing Technique

1. Sit comfortably with your back straight.

2. Inhale quietly through your nose for a count of four.

3. Hold your breath for a count of seven.

4. Finally, exhale completely through your mouth for a count of eight.

5. Repeat this cycle three more times. This technique helps to regulate your breath, slow your heart rate, and reduce anxiety, making it an excellent tool for stress management.

Additionally, incorporating the breath techniques with mindful movements like the seated spinal twist or shoulder shrug can create a sense of calm and focus, allowing you to tackle your tasks more efficiently and clearly.

By identifying opportunities for somatic breaks, incorporating desk-based movements, and employing effective stress management techniques, you can transform your workday into a more balanced and fulfilling experience.

3.2 Quick Somatic Routines for Morning Energy

Imagine starting your day with vitality and readiness rather than dragging yourself out of bed. Incorporating energizing somatic exercises into your morning routine can transform that morning sluggishness into vibrant energy. These exercises are not about going through the motions but feeling the immediate benefits.

Begin with a **simple standing stretch**.

1. Stand with your feet hip-width apart. As you inhale, reach your arms overhead, stretching from your fingertips to your toes.

2. Hold for a few seconds, feeling the length of your spine and the expansion in your ribcage.

3. Slowly exhale as you bring your arms back down. This stretch wakes your muscles and enhances blood circulation, boosting natural energy.

Simple Standing Stretch

Another excellent movement is the **dynamic forward fold**.

1. Stand with your feet together and inhale deeply. Extend your arms to the sky for a simple standing stretch.

2. As you exhale, hinge at your hips and fold forward, allowing your head and arms to hang heavy.

3. Inhale as you roll back up to a standing position, vertebra by vertebra. Repeat this movement a few times, focusing on the flow of your breath and the gentle stretch in your hamstrings and lower back.

4. This exercise helps to release any residual tension from sleep, invigorating your body and mind.

5. **Modification**: If your hamstrings are tight and your hands cannot reach the ground, you can use a chair or yoga blocks for support. Alternate bending your knees left and right as your hamstrings loosen.

Hinge at the Hips

Dynamic Forward Fold

Integrating somatic exercises with other morning activities can further enhance efficiency and effectiveness. For instance, perform a **gentle standing hip opener** while brushing your teeth for a few moments.

1. Stand with your feet hip-width apart and place your hands on your hips.

2. Inhale, lift one knee to a single-leg stand.

3. Exhale and slowly rotate your hips clockwise and counterclockwise in a circular motion. This movement helps to loosen the hip joints and improve flexibility.

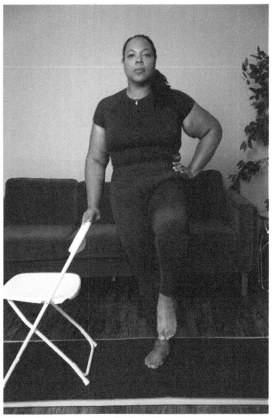

Single Leg Stand

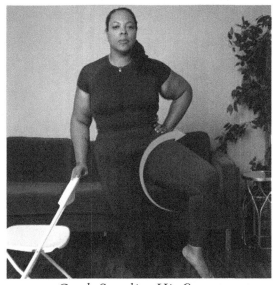

Gentle Standing Hip Opener

Similarly, you can practice mindful breathing while taking a shower. As you stand under the warm water, focus on deep, **diaphragmatic breaths**, allowing the steam to relax your muscles. These small integrations make it easier to maintain your routine, even on the busiest of mornings. Starting your day with a mindful routine can set a positive tone for everything that follows. Imagine waking up and gently easing your body into movement instead of rushing through your morning. A simple sequence of somatic exercises can energize and prepare your body for the day ahead.

Try It Yourself: Morning Routine

1. Begin with a **gentle spinal roll**:

    a. Stand up straight with your feet hip-width apart.

    b. Slowly roll your spine downwards, vertebra by vertebra, until your hands reach the floor.

    c. Allow your head to hang heavy, and take a few deep breaths in this position.

    d. Then, gradually roll back up, feeling each vertebra stack upon the next. This movement helps awaken the spine and release stiffness from the night.

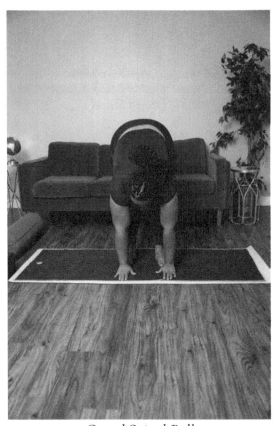

Gental Spinal Roll

Option with Blocks

1. Continue with a **side body stretch** to invigorate the muscles along your torso.

   a. Stand with your feet together and raise your arms overhead.

   b. Clasp your left wrist with your right hand and gently pull your left arm to the right, creating a stretch along the left side of your body.

   c. Hold for a few breaths and repeat on the other side.

   d. This stretch not only wakes the body but also encourages a full range of motion in the spine and shoulders, preparing you for the day's activities.

2. Transition into a **gentle seated hip opener** to further energize the body.

   a. Sit on the floor with your legs extended in front of you.

   b. Bend your right knee and place your right foot inside your left thigh.

   c. Inhale deeply, and as you exhale, hinge forward from the hips, reaching towards your left foot.

   d. Hold this position for a few breaths, feeling your hamstring and hip stretch. Repeat on the other side. This exercise helps release tension in the hips and lower back, which often become tight from prolonged sitting.

Starting position - Gental Seated Hip Opener

Gental Seated Hip Opener

Aligning your morning somatic practices with daily intentions or goals can also set a positive tone for the day. Before you begin your exercises, take a moment to think about what you want to achieve that day. Whether staying focused during meetings, being more patient with your kids, or simply maintaining a positive attitude, setting an intention can give your practice a sense of purpose. Remember that intention as you move through your exercises, allowing the movements to reinforce your goals. This alignment can help you start your day with clarity and motivation, enhancing your overall well-being.

3.3 Evening Somatic Wind-Down Practices

Creating a routine that promotes relaxation can improve sleep transition as the day winds down. Evening somatic exercises prepare your body and mind for rest, helping to melt away the stress and tension accumulated throughout the day. One gentle floor-based stretch that works wonders is the **Child's Pose**.

Try it Yourself: Child's Pose

1. Start kneeling on the floor with your big toes touching and knees spread apart.

2. Sit back on your heels and stretch your arms forward, lowering your torso between your thighs.

3. Rest your forehead on the ground and take deep breaths. This pose releases tension in the lower back and hips while the forward folding motion calms the mind.

4. **Modification**: Option to use a pillow or Bolster under your chest and head

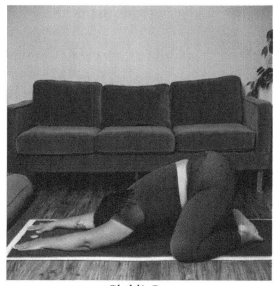

Child's Pose

Another effective evening exercise is the **Reclining Bound Angle Pose**.

Try it Yourself: Reclining Bound Angle Pose

1. Lie on your back and bring the soles of your feet together, allowing your knees to fall open to the sides.

2. Place your arms comfortably by your sides or overhead.

3. Close your eyes and breathe deeply, feeling the stretch in your inner thighs and groin.

4. This pose helps open the hips and release tension, promoting relaxation and preparing the body for sleep.

Reclined Bound Angle with blocks

Creating a calming evening routine is about more than just the exercises themselves; it's about setting the stage for relaxation.

Try It Yourself: Evening Routine

1. Start by establishing a consistent time each evening to practice your somatic exercises. This will signal to your body that it's time to wind down.

2. Begin with a few minutes of deep breathing to center yourself.

3. Follow this with gentle stretches like the **Child's Pose** and **Reclining Bound Angle Pose**.

4. Finish with a relaxation technique such as **progressive muscle relaxation**, in which you systematically tense and release each muscle group in your body, starting from your toes and working up to your head.

5. This routine helps to release physical tension and quiet the mind, making it easier to drift off to sleep.

The quality of your sleep is closely linked to your evening practices. You can improve sleep quality by incorporating somatic exercises into your nighttime routine. These exercises help to reduce physical tension, allowing your muscles to relax fully. Additionally, the mindful focus on your breath and body calms the mind, reducing the racing thoughts that often keep you awake at night. Over time, you'll fall asleep quickly and enjoy deeper, more restorative sleep.

As the day winds down, an evening routine of calming somatic exercises can help relax your body and mind, promoting better sleep.

Try It Yourself: Evening Routine

Start with a **gentle seated forward fold**.

1. Sit with your legs extended straight in front of you.

2. Inhale deeply, and as you exhale, slowly fold forward, reaching towards your toes.

3. Allow your head to drop and your back to round, creating a soothing stretch along your spine and hamstrings.

4. Hold this position for several breaths, focusing on releasing tension from the day.

Seated Forward Fold

Next, move into a **reclining twist** to further relax the body.

1. Lie on your back with your knees bent and feet flat on the floor.

2. Extend your arms out to the sides in a T-shape.

3. Inhale deeply, and as you exhale, lower your knees to the right, allowing your left hip to lift off the floor.

4. Turn your head to the left, creating a gentle twist in your spine.

5. Hold for a few breaths and repeat on the other side. This twist helps to release tension in the lower back and hips, promoting relaxation.

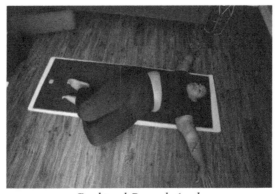

Reclined Bound Angle

Finally, conclude your evening routine with a simple **leg-up-the-wall pose.**

1. Lie on your back with your legs extended up a wall, forming an L-shape with your body.

2. Allow your arms to rest by your sides, palms facing up.

3. Close your eyes and take several deep breaths, feeling the gentle inversion soothe your nervous system.

4. This pose encourages blood flow from the legs to the heart, reducing swelling or fatigue in the lower limbs and preparing your body for restful sleep.

Legs up the wall

To enhance the relaxation effect, consider the environment in which you practice your evening routine. Dim lighting is critical to creating a soothing atmosphere. Use soft, warm lights or candles to create a tranquil setting. Ensure the room is quiet, or play gentle, calming music or nature sounds to help you relax. Aromatherapy can also be beneficial; scents like lavender and chamomile are known for their calming properties and can help you unwind. Keep your space clutter-free to avoid distractions, allowing you to focus entirely on your practice.

Integrating these relaxation-focused exercises into a calming evening routine allows you to get better sleep and a more restful night. This practice prepares your body for rest and signals to your mind that it's time to let go of the day's stress, making it easier to enjoy a peaceful, rejuvenating sleep.

3.4 Somatic Exercises While Traveling

Traveling can be a mixed bag of excitement and stress, often accompanied by the physical discomfort of cramped airline seats and long waits. Incorporating somatic exercises into your travel routine can make a significant difference. The beauty of somatic exercises is their portability; they require minimal space and no special equipment, making them perfect for hotel rooms or small spaces. One such exercise is the **seated cat-cow stretch**.

Try It Yourself: Seated Cat-Cow Stretch

1. Sit on the edge of your bed or a chair with your feet flat on the floor.

2. Place your hands on your knees.

3. As you inhale, arch your back, lift your chest, and look up.

4. As you exhale, round your spine, tucking your chin to your chest.

5. This movement helps to release tension in your spine and improve flexibility, perfect for shaking off the stiffness of a long journey.

Cow Strecth

Cat Stretch

Jet lag is another common issue that can throw your body's clock off balance. Specific somatic movements can help reset your body's internal clock and mitigate the effects of jet lag. The **standing forward fold** is particularly effective.

Try It Yourself: Standing Forward Fold

1. Stand with your feet hip-width apart. Inhale and extend your hands to the sky for a standing stretch.

2. Exhale and slowly bend forward at the hips, allowing your arms and head to hang down. This pose increases blood flow to your brain, helping to wake you up if you've just arrived in a new time zone.

3. **Modification**: If your arms don't reach the floor, you can support your hands and weight by using yoga blocks or small boxes under your hands.

Standing Stretch

Foward Fold With Blocks for support

Pair this with some **gentle ankle circles** to stimulate circulation in your legs.

Try It Yourself: Gentle Ankle Circles

1. Sit on the edge of your bed and extend one leg.

2. Rotate your ankle in slow circles, first clockwise, then counterclockwise.

3. Repeat with the other leg. These simple movements can help you feel more grounded and alert.

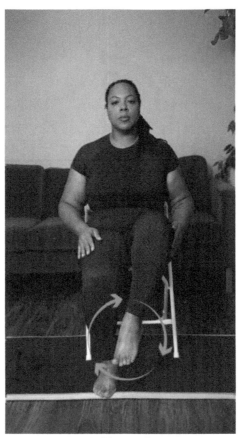

Ankle Circles

Integrating somatic exercises into your travel schedule is more manageable. Use layovers to your advantage by incorporating standing stretches or gentle walks around the terminal. On the plane, take a few moments every hour to do seated exercises like **shoulder shrugs** or **ankle circles** to keep your blood flowing and reduce stiffness. After long periods of sitting, whether on a plane or in a car, a quick series of somatic stretches can rejuvenate your body. For instance, practice the **seated spinal twist** while waiting for your luggage.

Try It Yourself: Seated Spinal Twist

1. Sit upright in your seat, Inhale, and place your right hand on the back of the seat.

2. Exhale, twist your torso to the right, holding for a few breaths.

3. Repeat on the other side to help release tension in your spine and improve mobility.

Seated Spinal Twist

Travel can be stressful, but somatic techniques can help reduce travel-related stress and anxiety. Deep **diaphragmatic breathing** is a powerful tool.

Try It Yourself: Diaphragmatic Breathing Exercise

1. Find a quiet spot, sit comfortably, and place one hand on your abdomen.

2. Inhale deeply through your nose, allowing your abdomen to rise,

3. Then, exhale slowly through your mouth. This type of breathing activates the parasympathetic nervous system, promoting relaxation and reducing anxiety.

Another helpful technique is the **body scan**.

Try it Yourself: Body Scan Exercise

1. Close your eyes and mentally scan your body from head to toe, noting any areas of tension.

2. Breathe deeply into those areas, consciously releasing the tension with each exhale.

3. This practice can be remarkably calming if you feel anxious about flying or navigating a busy airport.

3.5 Integrating Mindfulness with Somatic Movements

At its core, mindfulness is about being fully present in the moment, paying attention to your thoughts, feelings, and bodily sensations without judgment. When applied to somatic exercises, mindfulness enhances the effectiveness of each movement by fostering a deeper connection between your mind and body. Imagine moving through a series of gentle stretches while consciously focusing on your breath and the sensations in your muscles. This heightened awareness allows you to perform each exercise with greater precision and intention, maximizing the benefits and promoting a sense of inner calm.

To maintain mindfulness during somatic exercises, start by focusing on your breath. As you move, synchronize each inhale and exhale with your movements. For instance, when performing a simple neck roll, inhale as you tilt your head to one side and exhale as you bring it back to the center. This practice helps to regulate your breathing and keeps your mind focused on the present moment, reducing distractions and enhancing concentration. Another technique is to pay close attention to the bodily sensations during each movement. Notice the stretch in your muscles, the release of tension, and the energy flow through your body. By tuning into these sensations, you cultivate a more profound sense of body awareness, making each exercise more meaningful and effective.

Integrating mindfulness with somatic movements offers compounded benefits that go beyond physical well-being. One of the most significant advantages is more profound relaxation. When you perform somatic exercises mindfully, you engage the parasympathetic nervous system, promoting rest and relaxation. This helps to reduce stress and anxiety, leaving you more at ease. Additionally, mindful movement enhances body awareness, allowing you to detect and release tension before it becomes chronic. Over time, this increased awareness can improve your posture, coordination, and overall sense of physical well-being. Furthermore, mindfulness helps to quiet the mind, reducing mental clutter and promoting a sense of clarity and focus.

Combining practical somatic movements with mindfulness practices can easily be incorporated into your daily routine. One such exercise is the mindful body scan.

Try it Yourself: Body Scan Exercise

1. Lie down in a comfortable position and close your eyes.

2. Begin by focusing on your breath, taking slow, deep inhales and exhales. Gradually shift your attention to different body parts, starting with your toes and working your way up to your head.

3. As you focus on each area, notice any sensations of tension or discomfort and consciously release them with each exhale. This exercise promotes relaxation and enhances body awareness, making it an excellent way to start or end your day.

Another effective practice is the **mindful walking meditation**.

Try it Yourself: Mindful Walking Meditation.

1. Find a quiet space where you can move around without distractions.

2. As you begin to walk, pay attention to the sensations in your feet as they contact the ground. Notice the shifting of your weight, the movement of your legs, and the rhythm of your breath.

3. Focus on the present moment, allowing any thoughts or distractions to pass without judgment. This exercise helps to ground you in the present, reducing stress and promoting a sense of calm and clarity.

By seamlessly integrating mindfulness with somatic movements, you can transform your exercise routine into a holistic practice that nurtures your body and mind. This approach enhances the physical benefits of somatic exercises. It promotes mental and emotional well-being, helping you navigate daily challenges with greater ease and resilience.

Chapter 4: Enhancing Physical Health Through Somatics

Imagine waking up one morning and feeling a profound sense of ease in your body—a sensation you haven't experienced in years. Your joints move smoothly, your muscles feel relaxed, and the lingering aches and pains diminish. This transformation begins with understanding the fundamentals of somatic stretching. This practice prioritizes internal awareness and gentle movement to extend your range of motion.

4.1 Fundamentals of Somatic Stretching

Somatic stretching is distinct from traditional stretching due to its core principles. Traditional stretching often involves pushing the body to its limits, aiming for maximum flexibility through static or dynamic holds. In contrast, somatic stretching emphasizes internal awareness, allowing you to tune into your body's sensations and movements. This practice is about listening to your body and responding to its needs rather than forcing it into predetermined shapes. By focusing on gentle, mindful movements, you can safely extend your range of motion without risking injury.

One fundamental somatic stretch is the **seated hamstring stretch**.

Try it Yourself: Seated Hamstring Stretch

1. Sit on the floor with one leg extended and the other bent, foot against your inner thigh.

2. Inhale, extend your arms to the sky.

3. Exhale, slowly hinge at your hips, reaching towards your extended foot.

4. Rather than forcing the stretch and grabbing your foot, focus on the sensations in your hamstring and breathe deeply. Hold for several breaths, then inhale and raise your chest.

5. Switch legs and repeat. This stretch engages large muscle groups, promoting flexibility and relaxation.

Seated Hamstring Stretch with Yoga Strap

Another essential stretch is the **gentle neck release**.

Try it Yourself: Gentle Neck Release Exercise

1. Sit comfortably, inhale, and roll your shoulders back and down.

2. Exhale, drop your right ear towards your right shoulder, feeling the stretch along the left side of your neck.

3. Hold a few breaths, inhale back to center, then repeat on the other side.

4. These stretches are not about reaching a specific position but about experiencing the movement and releasing tension.

Gentle Neck Release

As you move, pay attention to how each stretch feels. Notice the areas of tightness and breath into them, allowing your body to relax. This mindful approach not only improves physical flexibility but also promotes mental calmness. For example, while performing the seated hamstring stretch, focus on the breath and the gentle sensations in your muscles. This practice shifts your attention from external goals to internal experiences, fostering a more profound sense of body awareness.

Building a daily stretching routine that fits your schedule is crucial for long-term mobility enhancement. Start by setting aside just 10-15 minutes each day. You might begin your morning with gentle stretches to wake your body or incorporate them into your evening routine to unwind. Consistency is key. By making stretching a regular part of your day, you reinforce positive movement patterns and maintain flexibility. Gradually, you can expand your routine to include more stretches, adapting it to your evolving needs. Whether at home, work, or traveling, these exercises can be easily integrated into your daily life, giving you the power to stay flexible and pain-free.

Try It Yourself: Daily Stretching Routine

1. **Seated Hamstring Stretch**: 2 minutes per leg

2. **Gentle Neck Release**: 1 minute per side

3. **Child's Pose**: 3 minutes

4. **Cat-Cow Stretch**: 2 minutes

5. **Shoulder Rolls**: 1 minute

Understanding and practicing these principles can significantly enhance your physical health through somatic stretching.

4.2 Somatic Exercises for Chronic Pain Management

Chronic pain is a complex condition that goes beyond mere physical discomfort. It affects your daily life, emotional well-being, and overall quality of life. Unlike acute pain, chronic pain persists for months or years, often outlasting the initial injury or underlying condition. This lingering pain is frequently linked to muscle memory and habitual tension patterns that become ingrained in your body over time. Somatic exercises offer a unique approach to addressing chronic pain by targeting these deep-seated issues. These exercises work at the root cause of pain by reprogramming muscle memory and reducing habitual tension rather than merely alleviating symptoms. This approach involves slow, mindful movements that help your body relearn how to move freely and without discomfort, offering a hopeful path to relief.

The **shoulder roll** is one of the most effective somatic exercises for pain relief.

Try it Yourself: Shoulder Roll Exercise

1. Stand or sit comfortably with your arms relaxed by your sides.

2. Inhale, slowly lift your shoulders towards your ears.

3. Exhale, roll them back and down in a circular motion.

4. Repeat this movement several times, focusing on the sensations in your shoulder muscles. This exercise helps to release built-up tension in the shoulders, a common area of chronic pain, especially for those who spend long hours at a desk.

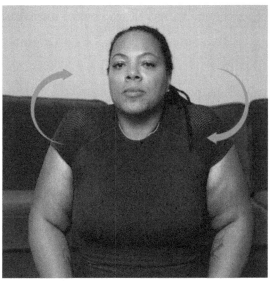

Shoulder Roll

Another helpful exercise is the **pelvic clock**.

Try it Yourself: Pelvic Clock Exercise

1. Lie on your back with your knees bent and feet flat on the floor. Imagine a clock on your lower abdomen.

2. Inhale, and slowly tilt your pelvis forward.

3. Exhale and rotate your pelvis in a circular motion from 12 o'clock to 3, 6, 9, and back to 12. This gentle movement targets the lower back and hips, often plagued by chronic pain, and promotes flexibility and relaxation.

Incorporating these exercises into your daily routine can make a significant difference in managing chronic pain. Start by setting a few minutes each morning and evening for somatic practice. For example, you can perform shoulder rolls while dressing in the morning to brew or do the pelvic clock exercise before bed. Consistency is key. Over time, these small, regular sessions can reduce pain and improve your overall mobility.

Additionally, consider integrating somatic exercises into your workday. Take short breaks to perform simple movements like neck stretches or seated spinal twists. These brief interludes can relieve tension and prevent pain from building up throughout the day.

Monitoring your body's response to these exercises is crucial for maximizing their effectiveness. Pay close attention to how your body feels before, during, and after each exercise. Adjust the movement or reduce its intensity if you notice any discomfort or pain. The goal is to move gently and mindfully without causing additional strain. Keep a journal to track your progress and document any changes in your pain levels. This practice can help you identify the most beneficial exercises and adjust your routine. By being attuned to your body's needs, you can prevent overexertion and ensure that your somatic practice remains a safe and effective tool for pain management.

4.3 Enhancing Joint Mobility with Gentle Movements

Healthy joints are the unsung heroes of our daily lives, allowing us to move easily and perform everyday activities without discomfort. When our joints are functioning well, we don't often think about them. But when stiffness or pain sets in, it can significantly impact our quality of life. Joint health is crucial for overall mobility, enabling us to walk, bend, lift, and twist without pain. Somatic exercises play a vital role in maintaining joint health by preventing stiffness and degradation through gentle, mindful movements that enhance flexibility and range of motion.

For the hips, one effective somatic movement is the **hip circles**.

Try it Yourself: Hip Circles Exercise

1. Stand with your feet shoulder-width apart and place your hands on your hips.

2. Inhale and exhale as you slowly rotate your hips in a circular motion, first clockwise and then counter-clockwise. This movement helps to lubricate the hip joints and increase their flexibility.

3. **Modification**: If you have limited mobility, perform the hip circles while seated

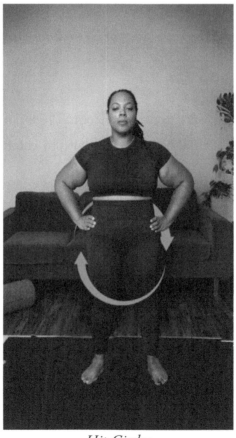

Hip Circles

For the knees, try the **seated knee extensions**.

Try it Yourself: Seated Knee Extensions

1. Sit on a chair with your feet flat on the ground.

2. Inhale, slowly extend one leg until it is straight, exhale, and lower it back down.

3. Repeat this movement several times on each leg. This exercise strengthens the muscles around the knee, supporting joint stability.

4. **Modification**: use a yoga strap, resistance band, or belt for added support if needed.

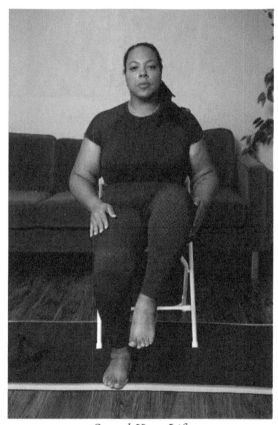

Seated Knee Lift

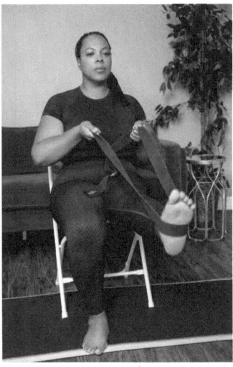

Knee Extension with Yoga Strap

For the shoulders, the **arm circles** are beneficial.

Try it Yourself: Arm Circles Exercise

1. Stand or sit with your arms extended to the sides.

2. Inhale and exhale as you slowly make small circles with your arms, gradually increasing the size of the circles as you inhale and exhale. This movement helps to improve shoulder mobility and reduce stiffness.

3. **Modification**: continue with smaller movements and gradually increase the range as your flexibility improves.

Arm Circles

Start your morning with a few hip circles to wake up your joints. Take short breaks throughout the day to perform seated knee extensions and arm circles. Consistency is critical to maintaining and enhancing joint mobility. Incorporating these gentle movements into your daily routine allows you to keep your joints flexible and pain-free.

4.4 Somatic Techniques for Back Pain Relief

Back pain is widespread and can stem from various causes, including poor posture, muscle imbalances, and stress. The spine is a complex bone, muscle, and ligament structure that provides support and flexibility. However, when specific muscles become overly tight or weak, they can pull on the spine, leading to misalignment and discomfort. For instance, prolonged sitting often results in tight hip flexors and a weak core, contributing to lower back pain. Understanding these muscular patterns is crucial in addressing back pain effectively.

Specific somatic exercises can target the spine and surrounding muscles to alleviate back pain and enhance spinal mobility. One effective movement is the "pelvic clock," performed by lying on your back with your knees bent and feet flat on the floor.

Try it Yourself: Pelvic Clock Exercise

1. Imagine a clock on your lower abdomen.

2. Inhale, slowly tilt your pelvis forward. Exhale as you move your pelvis in a circular motion, from 12 o'clock to 3, 6, 9, and back to 12.

3. This gentle movement helps release tension in the lower back and hips.

Another beneficial exercise is the "cat-cow stretch."

Try it Yourself: Cat-Cow Stretch

1. Start on all fours with your wrists under your shoulders and knees under your hips.

2. Inhale as you arch your back, lifting your head and tailbone (cow).

3. Exhale as you round your spine, tucking your chin and tailbone (cat). This flow increases spinal flexibility and reduces stiffness.

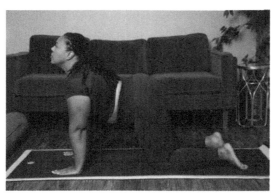

Cow Position

Cat Position

Daily Back Pain Relief Stretching Routine

1. **Pelvic Clock**: 3 minutes per leg

2. **Cat-Cow Stretch**: 3 minutes

3. **Child's Pose**: 3 minutes

4. **Spinal Twist**: 4 minutes

Gradually extend the duration as your flexibility improves. This routine not only addresses immediate discomfort but also promotes long-term spinal health. Many individuals have found relief through regular somatic practice. Take Sarah, a 52-year-old nurse who struggled with chronic lower back pain for years. After integrating somatic exercises into her daily routine, she noticed a substantial reduction in pain and increased mobility. Similarly, John, a 45-year-old office worker, discovered that these gentle movements relieved his persistent upper back tension, allowing him to work more comfortably and with less stress. These success stories highlight the transformative impact of somatic techniques on back pain management.

4.5 Exercises for Improving Posture and Balance

You might not realize it, but your posture and balance are crucial to your health. When your posture is aligned, your body functions more efficiently, reducing the risk of injury and enhancing bodily functions like digestion and circulation. Conversely, poor posture can lead to muscle strain, joint pain, and even breathing difficulties. Balance is equally important, especially as we age. Improved balance helps prevent falls and keeps your movements smooth and coordinated.

Core somatic exercises are essential for maintaining an upright and balanced posture. One effective exercise is the **pelvic tilt**.

Try it Yourself: Pelvic Tilt Exercise

1. Lie on your back with your knees bent and feet flat on the floor.

2. Slowly tilt your pelvis upward, pressing your lower back into the floor, then release.

3. This movement strengthens the lower abdominal muscles, which support your spine.

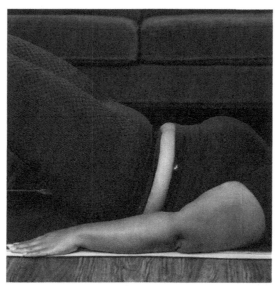

Pelvic Tilt

Another foundational exercise is the **cat-cow stretch**, performed on all fours.

Try it Yourself: Cat-Cow Stretch

1. Inhale, Arch your back, and bring your gaze towards the ceiling.

2. Exhale, round your back, and bring your chin towards your chest, syncing the movement with your breath.

3. This stretch improves spinal flexibility and engages the core muscles, which are crucial for maintaining good posture.

Balance-enhancing routines are vital for everyone but become increasingly important as we age. A simple yet effective routine is the **single-leg stand**.

Try it Yourself: Single Leg Stand Exercise

1. Inhale, raise one knee towards your chest, and stand on one leg.

2. Exhale release and lower the foot towards the ground.

3. Gradually increase the duration as your balance improves.

4. **Modification**: Hold onto a chair for support while you hold your elevated leg.

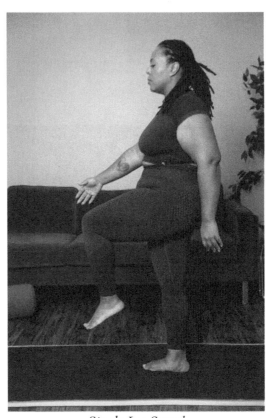

Single Leg Stand

Another beneficial exercise is the **heel-to-toe walk**.

Try it Yourself: Heel-to-toe Walk

1. Walk in a straight line, placing the heel of one foot directly in front of the toes of the other.

2. These exercises enhance proprioceptive abilities, helping you maintain stability and coordination in your daily activities.

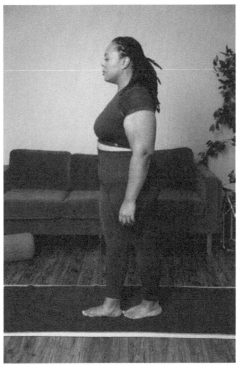

Heel to Toe Walk

Heel-to Toe Walk

Try It Yourself: Daily Posture and Balance Routine

1. **Pelvic Tilt**: 3 minutes

2. **Cat-Cow Stretch**: 3 minutes

3. **Single Leg Stand**: 1 minute on each side

4. **Heel-to-toe walk**: 3 minutes

Tracking your progress in posture and balance can be rewarding. Start by taking note of your current posture and balance abilities. Use a mirror to check your alignment, or ask a friend to observe. Over time, you'll notice improvements in how you stand and move. Adjust your routines as needed, increasing the difficulty or duration of exercises to continue challenging yourself. Keep a journal to document your progress, including any changes or improvements.

4.6 Strengthening Exercises Without Strain

The Somatic approach to strengthening is all about gently and effectively engaging muscles. Unlike traditional strength training, which often involves lifting heavy weights or performing high-intensity exercises, Somatic strengthening focuses on mindful, controlled movements that build strength without causing strain. This method emphasizes internal awareness, helping you tune into your body's signals and engage muscles optimally. Moving slowly and deliberately can strengthen your muscles while minimizing the risk of injury and overexertion, making this approach suitable for all fitness levels.

The **Somatic Bridge** is one effective exercise combining strength-building with heightened bodily awareness.

Try it Yourself: Somatic Bridge Exercise

1. Begin by lying on your back with your knees bent and feet flat on the floor, hip-width apart.

2. Inhale, slowly lift your hips towards the ceiling, engaging your glutes and core. Pause at the top, paying attention to the sensations in your muscles.

3. Exhale and slowly lower your hips back down. Repeat this movement several times, focusing on the quality of each lift rather than the number of repetitions. This exercise strengthens the lower back, glutes, and hamstrings while promoting body awareness and control.

4. **Modification:** with a smaller range of motion or use a cushion or yoga block under the hips for support.

Somatic Bridge

Integrating a range of somatic exercises can tailor whole-body strength routines to various fitness levels. For a balanced routine, continue with the **wall push-up**.

Try it Yourself: Wall Push-up Exercise

1. Stand facing a wall, place your hands shoulder-width apart on the wall, and step back to create a slight incline.

2. Inhale, slowly bend your elbows, lowering your chest towards the wall,

3. Exhale and push back to the starting position. This exercise strengthens the chest, shoulders, and arms without putting excessive strain on the joints.

4. **Modification:** reduce the incline or perform the movement against a countertop.

Wall Push Ups - Arms Extended

Wall Push Ups - Arms bent

Another valuable addition is the **seated leg lift**.

Try it Yourself: Seated Leg Lift Exercise

    1. Sit on a chair with your back straight and feet flat on the floor.

    2. Inhale, slowly lift one leg, keeping it straight.

    3. Exhale, lower it back down, and repeat on the other side. This movement engages the quadriceps and core, enhancing overall stability.

    4. **Modification:** use a yoga strap or a belt around your foot for additional support.

4.7 Balancing Exercises for Stability and Coordination

Balance and coordination are vital in our daily lives, from walking and climbing stairs to carrying groceries and engaging in recreational activities. Good balance helps prevent falls and injuries, particularly as we age, while strong coordination ensures smooth, purposeful movements. Often overlooked, these aspects of physical health are crucial for maintaining independence and overall mobility. Imagine standing confidently on one leg while reaching for something on a high shelf or navigating uneven terrain without fear of stumbling. Enhancing balance and coordination can significantly improve your quality of life, making everyday activities more accessible and more enjoyable.

Somatic balancing techniques focus on slow, controlled movements that enhance your body's internal sense of stability. One effective exercise is the **single-leg stand**.

Try it Yourself: Single Leg Stand Exercise

    1. Stand near a wall or sturdy chair for support.

    2. Shift your weight onto one leg and slowly lift the opposite foot off the ground, balancing on the standing leg.

    3. Hold this position for 10-15 seconds, then switch legs. As you become more comfortable, try extending the duration or performing the exercise without support.

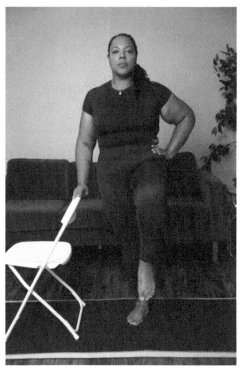

Single Leg Stand with Chair

Another helpful technique is the **slow, controlled walking pattern**.

Try it Yourself: Slow & Controlled Walking Pattern

1. Walk in a line, placing one foot before the other as if walking on a tightrope. This exercise challenges your balance and helps to strengthen the muscles that support stability.

Slow Controlled Walking

Coordination through somatic practices involves enhancing the neurological connections between your brain and body. When you perform mindful, deliberate movements, you engage your brain in a way that improves its communication with your muscles. For instance, a simple coordination exercise like **marching in place** while swinging your arms in opposite directions can significantly enhance these connections.

Try it Yourself: Marching in Place

1. Start by standing with your feet hip-width apart.

2. Lift your right knee while swinging your left arm forward, then switch to lifting your left knee and swinging your right arm. Inhale and exhale as you pace through the movement.

3. This cross-body movement helps to synchronize your brain and body, improving overall coordination.

March in Place

Incorporating balance exercises into your daily routine can be both practical and fun. Try balancing on one foot while brushing your teeth or standing on your toes while cooking. These small, consistent practices can significantly improve your balance over time. For example, practice the single-leg stand when waiting for your morning coffee to brew. Or, while watching TV, perform slow, controlled walking patterns during commercial breaks. Integrating these exercises into your everyday activities makes balance training an effortless part of your routine, leading to better stability and coordination in all aspects of your life.

4.8 Mobility Routines for Hip and Pelvic Health

The hip and pelvic areas are fundamental to our overall movement and stability. The hip joint, a ball-and-socket structure, allows for a wide range of motion—think of how you rotate, flex, and extend your legs. The pelvic region supports the spine and serves as an anchor for muscles and ligaments. Together, these areas enable us to walk, run, sit, and perform countless daily activities. Maintaining mobility here is crucial because stiffness or weakness can lead to compensatory patterns that cause pain and dysfunction elsewhere in the body.

To enhance hip and pelvic mobility, start with the **Cresent Lunge.**

Try it Yourself: Crescent Lunge

1. Stand with your feet hip-width apart,

2. Inhale, step one foot back into a lunge, and extend your arms to the sky, keeping your back leg straight and front knee bent.

3. Exhale, gently press your hips forward, feeling the stretch in your hip flexors. Hold for several breaths and switch sides.

Cresent Lunge

Another effective exercise is the **seated butterfly**.

Try it Yourself: Seated Butterfly

1. Sit on the floor with the soles of your feet together and knees bent outwards.

2. Hold your feet with your hands and gently press your knees towards the floor. This movement stretches the inner thighs and opens the hips, promoting flexibility and reducing tension.

3. **Modification**: Place yoga blocks or cushions under your knees to support your hips as they open. Remove

the block when you feel comfortable.

Maintaining hip and pelvic health has vast long-term benefits. Improved mobility in these areas can significantly reduce lower back pain, as flexible hips and a stable pelvis support better spinal alignment. Enhanced hip and pelvic strength also contribute to better posture, reducing the strain on other body parts. Over time, this can lead to a more balanced and pain-free life, allowing you to move with greater ease and confidence.

Customizing these routines for individual needs is essential to ensure everyone benefits. Use props like yoga blocks or cushions to support your movements if you have limited flexibility. For those with specific health conditions, such as hip arthritis, modify the intensity and range of motion to stay within a comfortable and pain-free zone. Listen to your body and adjust the exercises as needed, focusing on gentle, mindful movements that respect your limits.

4.9 Somatics for Longevity and Aging Well

As we age, our musculoskeletal health can face significant challenges. The natural aging process often brings about decreased bone density, muscle mass, and joint flexibility. These changes can lead to stiffness, pain, and an increased risk of injury. However, somatic exercises offer a way to mitigate these effects by focusing on gentle, mindful movements that improve overall physical health. These exercises enhance body awareness and promote proper movement patterns, which can help maintain muscle tone, flexibility, and balance.

Specific somatic exercises are particularly beneficial for older adults. One such exercise is the **seated spinal twist**, which can be done in a chair.

Try it Yourself: Seated Spinal Twist

1. Sit up straight with your feet flat on the floor.

2. Place your left hand on your right knee and your right hand on the back of the chair. Inhale deeply, then exhale as you gently twist your torso to the right.

3. Hold for a few breaths, exhaling to release. Then, switch sides. This exercise helps maintain spinal flexibility and relieve tension.

4. **Modification:** reduce the range of motion to stay within a comfortable zone.

Seated Spinal Twist

Another excellent exercise is the **standing calf raise**.

Try it Yourself: Standing Calf Raise

1. Stand with your feet hip-width apart.

2. Inhale, slowly lift your heels off the ground, balancing on the balls of your feet.

3. Hold for a few seconds, exhale lower your heels back down. This movement strengthens the calves and improves balance.

4. **Modification:** if standing calf raises are challenging, try them while holding onto a chair or wall for support.

Standing Calf Raise

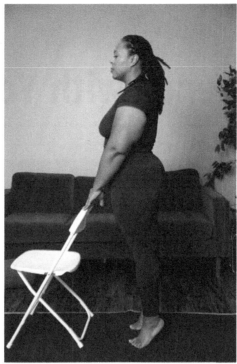

Standing Calf Raise with Chair Support

Using support tools like chairs, walls, and cushions can further enhance the safety and effectiveness of these exercises. For example, a cushion behind the lower back during seated exercises can provide additional support and comfort.

Integrating somatic exercises into daily life can be straightforward and highly beneficial. Older adults can incorporate these movements into their morning routine or as a part of their wind-down before bed. Consistency is crucial in reaping the benefits. Regularly engaging in somatic practice helps maintain mobility, reduce pain, and improve overall well-being. Additionally, building a community around somatic exercises can enhance motivation and enjoyment. Joining a local class or forming a small group with friends can provide social interaction and collective encouragement. Practicing together makes the experience more enjoyable and fosters community and support. When you're ready, we invite you to join our **Facebook Community** to support your practice.

As we look ahead, we'll explore how to tailor somatic exercises for specific health goals and create a holistic wellness plan incorporating these practices into every aspect of life.

Make a Difference with Your Review

"Health is Wealth."

Ancient Proverb

Imagine feeling stronger, calmer, and less stressed. Wouldn't that be great? My book, Somatic Exercise Made Simple, is all about that! It's filled with easy-to-follow exercises to help you feel better inside and out.

Would you like to help someone else feel better? By leaving a review, you can help others discover the power of somatic exercise and show them that this book can make a real difference in their lives.

Your review can help someone:

- Feel less pain.

- Reduce stress.

- Improve their mood.

- Move better.

- Sleep better.

I appreciate your kindness and am so grateful for your support. Together, we can help more people feel their best. – Dr. Danielle Griffin

Submit Your Book Review on Amazon

Chapter 5: Somatics for Mental and Emotional Well-being

Stress and anxiety are all too familiar to many of us. Picture this: you're sitting in traffic, already late for an important meeting, and you can feel your heart racing, your palms sweating, and your breath becoming shallow. This is a common scenario where anxiety takes hold, but what if I told you that the way you breathe can directly influence how you feel? Breathing is not just a biological necessity; it's a powerful tool that can help you manage emotional responses, especially anxiety.

5.1 Somatic Practices for Anxiety Reduction

Anxiety often manifests in the body as physical tension, creating a loop where physical discomfort feeds mental unease and vice versa. When you're anxious, your body tends to hold tension in specific areas like the chest and stomach, signaling your body's fight-or-flight response kicking in, preparing you for perceived threats by tightening muscles and quickening your breath. Somatic exercises help break this cycle by bringing your focus to these tension points and gently releasing them, restoring a sense of calm.

Consider these tailored movements when experiencing tight spots in the chest and stomach. One effective exercise is the **Chest Opener or Heart-Opening Stretch**.

Try it Yourself: Heart Opening Stretch

1. Stand with your feet hip-width apart and clasp your hands behind your back.

2. As you inhale, lift your chest and gently pull your shoulders back, opening up the front of your body.

3. Hold for a few breaths and release. This movement helps alleviate the tightness that often accompanies anxiety.

Heart Opening Stretch

Another helpful exercise is **Diaphragmatic breathing or Belly Breathing**.

1. Find a comfortable sitting or lying position. Place one hand on your chest and the other on your abdomen.

2. This simple act can soothe the stomach and calm your mind.

3. Inhale deeply through your nose, raising your abdomen while keeping your chest relatively still, using your diaphragm to breathe deeply.

4. Exhale slowly through your mouth, feeling your abdomen fall. Repeat this process for several minutes, focusing on the rise and fall of your abdomen. This technique promotes relaxation and increases oxygen intake, helping to calm your nervous system.

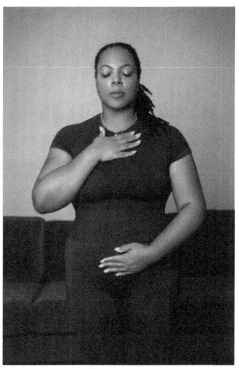

Belly Breathing

Try this guided somatic meditation incorporating gentle movements for a more profound experience.

Try it Yourself: Daily Practices for Anxiety Reduction

1. Begin by sitting or lying down in a comfortable position. Close your eyes and take a few deep breaths to center yourself.

2. Start with a **body scan**, mentally noting any areas of tension. As you identify these spots, incorporate gentle movements to release them. For instance, perform slow shoulder rolls if you notice tension in your shoulders. If your chest feels tight, do some **chest openers**.

3. Continue this process, moving through your body and pairing each area of tension with a corresponding movement. This practice relaxes your body and deepens your meditative state, enhancing your overall well-being.

A structured routine for managing anxiety can provide a reliable way to reduce acute symptoms and manage chronic levels.

1. Begin your day with a 5-minute body scan to identify and release tension.

2. Midday, take a break for some chest openers and belly breathing stretches to reset your nervous system.

3. In the evening, perform a guided somatic meditation to unwind and prepare for restful sleep.

Consistency is key, so aim to practice these exercises daily or whenever you feel anxiety creeping in. Combining mindfulness practices with somatic movements can enhance their effectiveness. When you focus on your breath and the sensations in your body, you create a powerful synergy that helps manage anxiety more efficiently. Mindfulness brings your attention to the present moment, reducing the mental chatter that often accompanies anxiety. Pair this with somatic movements, and you have a holistic approach that addresses both the mental and physical aspects of anxiety.

Consider the story of Jane, a 42-year-old nurse who struggled with chronic anxiety due to the high-stress nature of her job. Traditional treatments offered limited relief, so she turned to somatic exercises. By incorporating a daily routine of chest openers, belly breathing stretches, and guided somatic meditation, she noticed significant improvements in her anxiety levels. Combining mindfulness and movement helped her feel more grounded and in control, demonstrating the effectiveness of this approach in real-life anxiety management.

Understanding the connection between breath and emotion is crucial. When you're anxious, your body's sympathetic nervous system—responsible for the "fight or flight" response—kicks in, leading to rapid, shallow breathing, increased heart rate, and heightened muscle tension. Conversely, slow, deep breathing activates the parasympathetic nervous system, which promotes relaxation and calm - the essence of the breath-emotion connection; controlling your breath can influence your emotional state by directly affecting your nervous system.

Another effective method is **rhythmic breathing**, which helps stabilize emotions and maintain a calm mental state. One popular technique is the **4-7-8 Breath Technique**.

Try it Yourself: 4-7-8 Breath Technique

1. Begin by sitting comfortably with your back straight.

2. Inhale quietly through your nose for a count of four. Hold your breath for a count of seven. Finally, exhale completely through your mouth for a count of eight, making a whooshing sound.

3. Repeat this cycle three more times.

Rhythmic breathing helps regulate your breath, slow your heart rate, and reduce anxiety, making it an excellent tool for managing stress. Another technique is **box breathing.**

Try it Yourself: Box Breathing Technique

1. Find a comfortable sitting or lying position.

2. Inhale through your nose for four counts, holding for four, exhaling for four, and holding again for four.

This technique helps to reduce anxiety and restore calm quickly. These exercises can be beneficial during stressful public speaking or intense work meetings. Integrate these breathing techniques with somatic movements to target your physical, mental, and emotional needs for enhanced effectiveness.

Daily Routine: Diaphragmatic Breathing & Pelvic Tilt Exercise

1. Lie on your back with your knees bent and feet flat on the floor. Place your hands on your hips to feel the

movement.

2. As you inhale deeply through your nose, tilt your pelvis forward, arching your lower back slightly off the floor.

3. On the exhale, gently tilt your pelvis backward, pressing your lower back into the floor.

4. Repeat for 5-10 minutes, focusing on relieving lower back tension and promoting a sense of calm.

Daily Routine: Rhythmic Breathing & Spinal Twist Exercise

1. Find a comfortable seated position. Sit up straight in your chair with your feet flat on the floor

2. Place your right hand on the back of the chair and your left hand on your right knee.

3. Inhale deeply as you gently twist your torso to the right, hold your breath, and look over your right shoulder.

4. Exhale, release the twist. Focus on deep, rhythmic breathing. Repeat on the other side.

5. Alternate sides for 5-10 minutes, focusing on relieving tension in the spine and reducing anxiety.

By understanding the breath-emotion connection and practicing these techniques, you can effectively manage anxiety and promote well-being.

5.2 Exercises for Cultivating Positivity and Joy

When you're feeling down, the last thing you might think of is moving your body, but somatic exercises can be an excellent way to lift your spirits. One exercise that helps boost mood is the **Heart-Opening Stretch**.

Try it Yourself: Heart-Opening Stretch

1. Stand with your feet hip-width apart and clasp your hands behind your back.

2. As you inhale, lift your chest and gently pull your shoulders back, opening up the front of your body. This stretch relieves tension and encourages a sense of openness and positivity.

Another helpful exercise is the **Gentle Spinal Twist**.

Try it Yourself: Gentle Spinal Twist

1. Sit comfortably on the floor with your legs crossed.

2. Place your right hand on your left knee and your left hand behind you. Inhale deeply, then exhale as you

gently twist your torso to the left, looking over your shoulder.

3. Hold for a few breaths and repeat on the other side. This movement helps release tension in the spine and shoulders, promoting relaxation and well-being.

4. **Modification**: If sitting on the floor is unobtainable, do this exercise in a chair with your feet on the floor.

Gental Spinal Twist

Improving your posture through somatic exercises can profoundly impact your mood and self-esteem. When you stand tall with an open chest and relaxed shoulders, you signal to your brain that you're confident and in control, often called the "power pose." Practicing exercises that enhance posture, such as the **Wall Angel**, can help.

Try it Yourself: Wall Angels

1. Stand with your back against a wall, feet a few inches away, and your lower back gently pressing into the wall.

2. Raise your arms to shoulder height with elbows bent at 90 degrees, and slowly slide them up and down the wall, keeping them in contact with the surface.

3. This exercise strengthens the muscles that support good posture, improving mood and self-esteem.

Wall Angles - Starting Position

Wall Angles

Creating a joyful somatic routine involves incorporating movements that make you feel good and uplift your spirits.

Try it Yourself: Daily Routine for Positivity and Joy

    1. Start with a few minutes of gentle stretching to warm up your body.

2. Follow this with the **Heart-Opening Stretch** and the **Gentle Spinal Twist** to release tension and promote relaxation.

3. Add in some dynamic movements like the **Arm Swing**.

   a. Stand with your feet hip-width apart and swing your arms back and forth, allowing your body to sway naturally. This movement helps to release pent-up energy and induce feelings of happiness.

4. Finish with a few moments of stillness, standing or sitting quietly, and observing how your body feels. Do this routine in the morning to start your day on a positive note or in the evening to unwind.

Participating in group somatic sessions or classes can significantly enhance your sense of joy and connectivity. There's something incredibly uplifting about moving in unison with others and sharing the mindful movement experience. Look for local classes or gatherings that provide a supportive environment to connect with like-minded individuals, share your progress, and celebrate your achievements. The sense of community and collective energy can amplify the positive effects of somatic exercises, making them even more enjoyable and beneficial.

5.3 Somatic Practices to Enhance Emotional Awareness

Understanding how your body and mind reflect each other is a powerful tool for managing emotional well-being. Physical sensations often mirror emotional states, and somatic practices can help you become more aware of these subtle cues. When you're tense, your muscles tighten. When you're sad, you might feel a heaviness in your chest. These physical manifestations of emotions are your body's way of communicating with you. By paying closer attention to these signals, you can gain insight into your emotional state and take proactive steps to address it.

One effective way to heighten this awareness is through **body scanning**. This exercise involves mentally scanning your body from head to toe, noticing any areas of tension, discomfort, or unusual sensations.

Try it Yourself: Body Scanning

1. Start by finding a quiet space to sit or lie comfortably.

2. Close your eyes and take a few deep breaths to center yourself.

3. Focus your thoughts starting at the top of your head and slowly work your way down, paying attention to each part of your body and how it feels.

4. When you encounter an area of tension, take a moment to focus on it, breathe deeply, and consciously release the tension. This practice helps you identify where your body holds emotions and teaches you how to release them.

Mapping emotions in the body involves recognizing that emotions often reside in specific areas. For example, anxiety might manifest as tightness in the chest, while anger could show up as tension in the jaw or fists. To explore this, try a simple exercise:

1. Stand or sit comfortably and think about a recent emotional experience.

2. Notice where you feel the emotion in your body. Is it in your shoulders, your stomach, or perhaps your back?

3. Once you've identified the location, choose a few gentle somatic movements to release the tension. If you feel anxiety in your chest, try a gentle **chest-opening stretch**. Practice slow, mindful jaw movements if you feel angry and tense.

4. By connecting physical sensations with emotional states, you can better understand your emotions and how to manage them.

A **daily emotional awareness routine** can help maintain and enhance your emotional intelligence.

Try it Yourself: Daily Emotional Awareness Routine

1. Start your day with a few minutes of body scanning to check in with yourself. Notice how you feel and any areas of tension.

2. Throughout the day, take short breaks to perform somatic exercises that target these areas. For instance, if you notice tightness in your shoulders, do a few shoulder rolls. If you feel tension in your lower back, try gentle pelvic tilts.

3. End your day with another body scan to release accumulated tension and reflect on your emotional experiences while doing Legs up the Wall.

This routine helps you stay connected to your body and emotions, making it easier to manage stress and maintain emotional balance.

Take Sarah, a 38-year-old teacher who struggled with chronic anxiety. Through regular somatic exercises, she learned to identify the physical sensations associated with her anxiety, such as tightness in her chest and shoulders. By practicing body scanning and targeted movements, she was able to release this tension and significantly reduce her anxiety levels. Another example is Tom, a 50-year-old executive who dealt with chronic stress and anger. By mapping his emotions in his body, he discovered that his anger manifested as tension in his jaw and fists. Through somatic practices, he learned to relax in these areas, improving his emotional regulation and overall well-being.

Understanding how your body and mind reflect each other, practicing body scanning, mapping emotions, and incorporating a daily routine can significantly enhance your emotional awareness and well-being.

5.4 Using Somatics to Overcome Mental Fatigue

Mental fatigue can sneak up on you, gradually weakening your ability to focus, process information, and make decisions. Common signs include difficulty concentrating, frequent forgetfulness, irritability, and a general sense of being overwhelmed. Mental fatigue often stems from prolonged cognitive activity, stress, and inadequate rest. Your brain is running on fumes, struggling to meet daily demands. Recognizing these symptoms is the first step in addressing mental fatigue and finding ways to refresh and reset your mind.

Somatic exercises offer unique solutions to combat mental fatigue, providing quick resets for the mind and body. One effective technique is the **seated body scan**.

Try it Yourself: Seated Body Scan

1. Sit comfortably in a chair, feet flat on the ground and hands resting on your thighs. Close your eyes and take a few deep breaths to center yourself.

2. Begin by focusing on your toes and noticing any sensations or tension. Gradually move your attention up through your body—feet, ankles, calves, knees, thighs, hips, abdomen, chest, shoulders, arms, hands, neck, and head.

3. Spend a moment on each area, breathing deeply and consciously releasing any tension you encounter.

This exercise not only relaxes your body but also clears your mind, making it an excellent tool for moments of mental burnout. The standing stretch sequence is another powerful somatic reset.

Try it Yourself: Standing Stretch Sequence

1. Find a space where you can stand comfortably.

2. Inhale, extend your arms to the sky, exhale, lower your arms, and hinge at your hips to start a gentle forward fold. Allow your arms to hang down and your head lower towards the ground.

3. Take a few deep breaths in this position, feeling the stretch in your hamstrings and lower back. Grab your elbows with your opposite hands and find a gentle sway from left to right in a rag doll position.

4. Inhale, slowly roll up to a standing position, stacking each vertebra.

5. Next, reach your arms overhead, interlock your fingers, and stretch upwards, feeling the length of your spine.

6. Finish with a gentle side stretch—Exhale, leaning to the right. Inhale back to the center, exhale to the left, and inhale back to the center.

Do this sequence as often as needed to relieve physical tension, revitalize your mind, and help you return to your tasks with renewed focus.

Set reminders on your phone or computer to prompt you to take short breaks every hour. During these breaks, perform quick somatic exercises like the seated body scan or the standing stretch sequence. Even a few minutes of mindful movement can make a big difference in how you feel and perform. These small, consistent practices can help you maintain mental clarity and prevent burnout.

The long-term benefits of regular somatic practice extend beyond immediate relief. Over time, these exercises build mental stamina and resilience, making it easier to handle cognitive demands and stress. By incorporating somatic exercises into your daily routine, you train your mind and body to respond to stress more effectively, reducing the overall impact of mental fatigue. This ongoing practice fosters greater self-awareness, helping you recognize early signs of burnout and take proactive steps to address them. As a result, you'll find yourself better equipped to navigate the challenges of daily life with greater ease and efficiency.

5.5 Somatics for Deepening Sleep Quality

When nighttime rolls around, the state of relaxation in your body can dramatically affect how easily you fall asleep and the quality of your rest. Physical relaxation signals to your brain that it's safe to enter a state of rest, reducing the production of stress hormones like cortisol. Somatic exercises are practical in facilitating deep relaxation by helping you release physical and mental tension. They activate the parasympathetic nervous system, promoting calm and preparing your body for sleep, signaling the same system responsible for the "rest and digest" functions, making it easier to transition into a peaceful slumber.

Creating a pre-sleep somatic routine can enhance sleep quality. Start with a gentle **seated forward fold** to relax your spine and calm your mind.

Try it Yourself: Seated Forward Fold

1. Sit on the floor or the edge of your bed with your legs extended in front of you.

2. Inhale deeply, and extend your arms to the sky.

3. Exhale as you slowly fold forward, hinge at the hips, allowing your head and arms to lower towards your legs. Hold this position for several breaths, feeling the stretch in your hamstrings and lower back.

Next, move into a **reclining twist**.

Try it Yourself: Reclining Twist

1. Lie on your back with your knees bent and feet flat on the floor.

2. Inhale, extend your arms out to the sides.

3. Exhale, lower your knees to the right, turning your head to the left. Hold for a few breaths.

4. Inhale back to center, Exhale switch sides.

Reclining Twist Starting Position

Reclining Twist

Finish with a simple **legs-up-the-wall pose** to promote circulation and relaxation.

Try it Yourself: Legs-up-the-wall

1. Lie on your back with your legs extended up a wall, forming an L-shape with your body. Close your eyes and take several deep breaths, feeling the gentle inversion soothe your nervous system.

Legs Up the Wall

Optimizing your sleep environment is just as crucial as the exercises themselves. A comfortable, clutter-free bedroom can significantly affect how well you sleep. Start by ensuring your mattress and pillows provide adequate support. Soft, breathable bedding can also enhance comfort. Consider the lighting in your room; dim, warm lights or even candles can create a calming atmosphere. Consider using a white noise machine or earplugs if you're easily disturbed by sounds. The room temperature is another crucial factor; aim for a cool, comfortable setting to promote restful sleep. Aromatherapy can also be beneficial; scents like lavender and chamomile are known for their calming properties and can help you unwind.

Tracking your sleep patterns and quality improvements can provide valuable insights and motivate you. Keep a sleep journal where you note the time you go to bed, wake up, and the quality of your sleep. Record any nighttime awakenings and how you felt upon waking. Over time, you'll be able to identify patterns and see how the somatic exercises impact your sleep. You can also use sleep-tracking apps or devices to gather more detailed information. By consistently monitoring your sleep, you can adjust your routine and environment as needed, ensuring that you continue to enjoy the benefits of restful, restorative sleep.

5.6 Managing Grief and Emotional Pain Through Somatics

Grief is not just an emotional experience; it's a physical one too. When you're grieving, you might feel a tightness in your chest, a lump in your throat, or a heavy sensation in your limbs. These physical manifestations of grief are your body's way of expressing the deep emotional pain you're going through. Addressing these physical symptoms through somatic practice can be incredibly healing. Somatic exercises help you tune into your body, acknowledge where you're holding tension, and gently release it. This process can facilitate emotional healing and relieve the intense physical sensations of grief.

One effective exercise for emotional release is the **Heart-Opening Stretch**. This movement can help release the tightness often felt in the chest during periods of grief.

Try it Yourself: Heart-Opening Stretch

1. Stand with your feet hip-width apart and clasp your hands behind your back.

2. Inhale deeply, lifting your chest and gently pulling your shoulders back.

3. Hold this position for a few breaths, feeling the stretch across your chest and the opening of your heart area.

4. This exercise helps to release physical tension and encourages emotional openness, allowing you to process your grief more fully.

Another helpful exercise is the **Seated Forward Fold**.

Try it Yourself: Seated Forward Fold

1. Sit on the edge of your bed or the ground with your legs extended in front of you.

2. Inhale deeply, then exhale as you fold forward, allowing your head and arms to hang. This pose can help release the heaviness often felt in the body during grief, providing a sense of relief and comfort.

Seated Forward Fold

Supporting emotional recovery through somatic practices involves a holistic approach. Alongside regular somatic exercises, consider incorporating activities that promote overall well-being. Mindfulness meditation can be a powerful complement to somatic practices, helping you stay present and grounded. Spend a few minutes each day sitting quietly, focusing on your breath, and observing your thoughts and feelings without judgment. Journaling is another effective strategy. Writing down your thoughts and emotions can provide an outlet for your grief and help you process your feelings. Regular physical activity, such as walking or gentle yoga, can also support your emotional recovery by boosting your mood and reducing stress.

Connecting with supportive practices can enhance the healing process when used alongside somatic exercises. Counseling or therapy can provide a safe space to explore your feelings and receive professional guidance. Support groups offer a sense of community and understanding, allowing you to share your experiences with others going through similar journeys. Combining these practices with somatic exercises creates a comprehensive support system that addresses grief's physical and emotional aspects. Imagine attending a weekly therapy session where you discuss your feelings and then incorporating what you've learned into your somatic practice at home. This integrated approach can significantly enhance your healing process, providing immediate relief and long-term emotional support.

By understanding how grief manifests in the body and incorporating specific somatic exercises and complementary practices, you can support your emotional recovery and healing. These strategies help you navigate the complex landscape of grief, providing tools to manage emotional pain and facilitate a sense of well-being.

Chapter 6: Addressing Specific Health Goals

Imagine this:

> You've just had a particularly stressful day. Your shoulders are tight. Your head is throbbing. Your mind is spinning with a thousand thoughts. There's no escape, and the tension is almost unbearable.

This scenario is all too common, but what if there was a way to alleviate stress and find a sense of calm in the middle of your busy life? With their gentle yet powerful approach, somatic exercises can bring a profound sense of relief and calm, even amid a stressful day.

6.1 Customizing Your Routine for Immune and Nervous System Response

When you experience stress, your body reacts in immediate and profound ways. The sympathetic nervous system, responsible for the "fight or flight" response, kicks into high gear, releasing cortisol and adrenaline, hormones that prepare your body to confront or flee from a threat. You might notice your heart rate increasing, muscles tensing, and your breath becoming shallow. When stress becomes chronic, it can lead to various health issues.

Chronic stress has long-term effects that can significantly impact your health. Elevated cortisol levels over extended periods can contribute to hypertension, increasing your risk of heart disease. Digestive problems, such as irritable bowel syndrome (IBS), can also arise as stress disrupts the balance of gut bacteria and affects digestion. Moreover, chronic stress can suppress the immune system, making you more susceptible to infections and illnesses. It's a cascade of adverse effects that can deteriorate your overall well-being.

Somatic exercises are helpful for stress management because they help regulate your body's response. These exercises foster greater physiological awareness, allowing you to recognize and address tension before it escalates into chronic stress. By practicing mindful movement and controlled breathing, you can activate the parasympathetic nervous system, which promotes relaxation and counteracts the stress response. This balanced approach helps you maintain a state of calm and resilience, even in stressful situations.

Identifying your stress triggers is an essential step in managing stress effectively. Pay attention to the situations, people, or tasks that consistently cause you stress. Notice how your body reacts—do your shoulders tighten, your heart race, or do you feel a knot in your stomach? These physical manifestations are crucial indicators of stress. A stress journal can help identify patterns and triggers and provide valuable insights into your stress response.

Designing a personalized stress-relief routine involves selecting exercises that address your needs and triggers. This customization process empowers you to take control of your stress management, making you feel proactive and in charge of your well-being.

Try it Yourself: Daily Stress Relief Routine

Start by setting aside 10-15 minutes each day for your routine.

1. Begin with deep breathing exercises to center yourself. Inhale deeply through your nose, allowing your abdomen to rise, and exhale slowly through your mouth.

2. Follow this with gentle **neck rolls** to release shoulder and neck tension. Sit comfortably, drop your chin to your chest, and slowly roll your head in a circular motion.

3. Next, perform **pelvic tilts** to alleviate lower back tension. Lie on your back with your knees bent and feet flat on the floor. Tilt your pelvis forward on an inhale, arching your lower back slightly, and tilt it back on an exhale, pressing your lower back into the floor.

Quick somatic exercises, such as neck rolls or pelvic tilts, are practical for immediate stress relief. Combined with breathing patterns, such as **box breathing**, these exercises provide practical tools you can use anytime, anywhere, making you feel equipped and prepared to manage stress.

Try it Yourself: Box Breathing

1. Find a comfortable sitting or lying position.

2. Inhale through your nose for four counts, holding for four, exhaling for four, and holding again for four.

3. This technique helps to reduce anxiety and restore calm quickly. These exercises can be beneficial during stressful situations like public speaking or intense work meetings.

Take a few moments to step aside, perform these exercises, and return feeling more centered and composed. Long-term stress management through somatic practice involves consistent effort and mindfulness. Over time, regular practice can change how your body responds to stress, making you more resilient and adaptable. Monitor your response to these techniques and adjust as necessary. Keep track of what works best for you, and don't hesitate to modify your routine to fit your evolving needs. This ongoing practice helps you manage stress and enhances your overall well-being, leading to a healthier, more balanced life.

6.2 Somatic Exercises for Digestive Health

The relationship between your nervous system and digestive health is more intertwined than you might realize. The gut-brain axis is a complex communication network that links your central nervous system with your digestive tract. When stress activates the sympathetic nervous system, it can disrupt this communication, leading to digestive issues like bloating, constipation, or acid reflux. On the other hand, when the parasympathetic nervous system is engaged, it promotes relaxation and efficient digestion. Somatic exercises can foster this relaxation, improving gut mobility and overall digestive health.

Somatic exercises are beneficial for enhancing digestion. **Abdominal massages** are a simple yet powerful tool.

Try it Yourself: Abdominal Massages

1. Start by lying on your back with your knees bent.

2. Use your fingertips to gently massage your abdomen in a circular motion, moving clockwise.

3. This helps stimulate peristalsis—the wave-like muscle contractions that move food through your digestive tract.

Another beneficial exercise is the **seated twist**.

Try it Yourself: Seated Twist

1. Sit on the floor with your legs extended.

2. Bend your right knee and place your right foot outside your left thigh.

3. Inhale deeply, then exhale as you twist your torso to the right, placing your left elbow on the outside of your right knee for support.

4. Hold for a few breaths and repeat on the other side. This twist helps to massage the internal organs and improve digestion.

Seated Twist

A daily routine of somatic exercises can promote long-term digestive health and alleviate common issues.

1. Begin your day with a few minutes of abdominal massage to wake up your digestive system.

2. Follow this with seated twists to stimulate gut mobility.

3. After meals, practice deep diaphragmatic breathing to engage the parasympathetic nervous system and aid digestion.

4. In the evening, a gentle forward fold can help to relax your digestive tract and prepare your body for restful sleep.

Supporting digestive health goes beyond somatic exercises. Hydration is crucial, so drink plenty of water throughout the day to keep things moving smoothly. A fiber-rich diet of fruits and vegetables can also support healthy digestion. Stress management techniques like mindfulness and meditation can complement somatic exercises, helping to keep your nervous system balanced. Avoiding heavy, rich meals before bedtime and eating smaller, more frequent meals can prevent digestive discomfort. Combining these lifestyle tips with your somatic practice creates a holistic digestive health approach that supports your body and mind.

6.3 Somatics for Boosting Energy

Energy levels can swing throughout the day, influenced by your physical posture, breathing patterns, and mental state. Slouching at your desk can make you feel sluggish while standing tall and taking deep breaths can invigorate you. Your mental state plays a significant role, too; feeling overwhelmed can drain your energy, whereas a focused and calm mind can keep you energized. Understanding these fluctuations helps you take control of your energy, making it easier to maintain productivity and well-being.

Energizing somatic exercises enhance circulation and oxygenate the blood, giving you a natural boost. They include dynamic stretches like **arm swings.**

Try it Yourself: Arm Swings

1. Stand with your feet hip-width apart and swing your arms back and forth

2. Allow your body to sway naturally. This movement helps to release pent-up energy and induce feelings of happiness.

Arm Swings

Torso twists are another dynamic movement to get your blood flowing and wake up your muscles.

Try it Yourself: Torso Twists

1. Stand with your feet hip-width apart and elbows and hands at shoulder height.

2. Inhale, slowly twist your torso to the left, bring your gaze towards the back of the room, and lift your right heel off the ground. Exhale back to center.

3. Inhale, twist your torso to the right, bring your gaze towards the back of the room, and lift your left heel off the ground.

4. Exhale back to center. Repeat this exercise for 1-2 minutes and gradually increase your speed and rotation to a level you're comfortable with as you loosen the muscles and awaken your body.

Torso Twist

Another effective practice is invigorating breathwork, such as **bellows breath**.

Try it Yourself: Bellows Breath Technique

1. Sit comfortably, your jaw slightly open and your lips sealed closed. Inhale and exhale rapidly through your nose, keeping your breaths short and equal. This breathing pattern increases oxygen intake and stimulates your nervous system, leaving you feeling alert and refreshed.

Try it Yourself: Daily Energy Boost Routine

1. Morning is a great time to start. Begin with a few minutes of dynamic stretching like the **torso twist** or **dynamic forward fold** to shake off sleepiness right after you wake up. Finish with a **mindful meditation** to set a positive tone for the day.

2. Mid-morning is another ideal time when you might experience a dip in energy.

3. Take a short break to do some **invigorating breathwork**, which can help you regain focus and stamina.

4. In the afternoon, a quick session of **dynamic stretches** can counteract the post-lunch slump and energize you for the rest of the day.

Maintaining balanced energy levels throughout the day involves more than just sporadic bursts of activity. Consistent somatic practices can help you avoid mid-day slumps and fatigue. Incorporate short, regular breaks into your schedule to perform these exercises. For example, take a five-minute break every hour to stand up, stretch, and breathe deeply. This keeps your energy levels stable and prevents the build-up of tension and stress. By making these practices a regular part of your day, you ensure that your energy remains balanced, allowing you to stay productive and feel good from morning to night.

6.4 Creating a Calm Mind with Vagus Nerve Stimulation

When it comes to enhancing your parasympathetic response, advanced techniques for stimulating the vagus nerve can be incredibly effective. One such technique is the "**gargling exercise**." It might sound simple, but gargling with water engages the muscles at the back of your throat connected to the vagus nerve. Another method is "**humming**." By humming, you create vibrations that stimulate the vagus nerve, promoting a state of relaxation. Try humming a favorite tune or simply producing a steady hum for a few minutes. These exercises can be easily integrated into your daily routine, making them practical tools for maintaining a calm state of mind. If your mind is active from a busy work day, and you're having trouble falling asleep, try the "**Shhh**" sound. The same sound we often use to calm a crying baby calms our minds and prepares us for sleep. Try lying down, closing your eyes, and "shhh" yourself to sleep. Your mind begins to focus on the sound and calm the nervous system to prepare for sleep.

The health of your vagus nerve connects to your mental well-being. A well-functioning vagus nerve can help regulate your mood and reduce feelings of anxiety and stress. The vagus nerve plays a crucial role in the parasympathetic nervous system, responsible for the "rest and digest" functions. When stimulating the vagus nerve, it sends signals to your brain to release neurotransmitters like acetylcholine and serotonin, which help to calm your mind and improve your mood, making vagus nerve stimulation a powerful tool for managing anxiety and enhancing overall mental health.

To integrate these exercises into your daily routine, start with small, manageable steps. For instance, you can practice gargling each morning after brushing your teeth. You can humm during your commute or while preparing meals. Consistency is key, so aim to incorporate these exercises simultaneously each day to create a habit. Over time, you likely notice a cumulative effect. Maintaining a calm, balanced state becomes more accessible and more natural. These simple practices can significantly affect managing stress and maintaining mental clarity throughout the day.

Scientific studies support the effectiveness of vagus nerve stimulation through somatic practices. Research published in the journal *Frontiers in Psychology* found that vagus nerve stimulation can significantly reduce symptoms of depression and anxiety. Another study in the *Journal of Clinical Psychiatry* highlighted the benefits of vagus nerve stimulation for improving overall mood and emotional regulation. These findings underscore the power of somatic exercises in promoting mental health by enhancing vagus nerve function.

6.5 Somatic Yoga for Emotional Balance

Somatic yoga is a unique blend of traditional yoga and somatic principles, focusing on the internal experience of movement and sensation. Unlike conventional yoga, which often emphasizes achieving specific poses, somatic yoga prioritizes body awareness and emotional regulation. This practice encourages you to listen to your body, move mindfully, and connect with your inner self, facilitating a sense of emotional balance. Integrating somatic principles into yoga creates a physically beneficial practice and profound healing for your mind and emotions.

Some yoga poses naturally align with somatic principles, making them ideal for fostering emotional balance. One such pose is the **Cat-Cow stretch**.

Try It Yourself: Cat-Cow Stretch

1. Start on your hands and knees with your wrists directly under your shoulders and your knees under your hips in a tabletop position.

2. Inhale, and move into the Cow position by lifting your head and tailbone towards the ceiling.

3. On the exhale, transition into the Cat position by tucking your chin to your chest and drawing your navel towards your spine. Repeat this flow for several breaths, moving slowly and mindfully.

4. **Modification:** If kneeling is uncomfortable, you can sit on a chair. Place your hands on your knees, and as you inhale, arch your back and lift your chest. On the exhale, round your spine and tuck your chin.

Cow Pose

Cat Pose

Another beneficial pose is the **Child's Pose**.

Try it Yourself: Child's Pose

1. Kneel on the floor, sit back on your heels with the tops of your feet flat on the floor, and extend your arms forward.

2. Inhale, sit your hips back, exhale, and rest your forehead on the mat. This pose encourages a sense of surrender and calm, allowing you to release built-up tension and stress.

3. **Modification**: Rest your forehead on a yoga block or bring a pillow or bolster under your chest and head for support.

Child's Pose

Somatic yoga can release pent-up emotions through mindful movement and breath. When you practice somatic yoga, you engage in movements that gently stretch and open areas of your body where emotions might be stored. For instance, hip openers like **Pigeon Pose** can help release emotions held in the hips, a shared storage area for stress and anxiety.

Try it Yourself: Pigeon Pose

1. Start on your hands and knees. Make sure your hands are directly under your shoulders and your knees are directly under your hips.

2. Inhale, bring your right knee forward, and gently move your right knee towards your right wrist. Slide your right foot forward towards your left wrist. With your hips lifted and square towards the ground, slide and extend your left leg behind. Exhale, gently lower your upper body towards the floor.

3. You can rest your forehead on the ground. Hold the pose. Breathe deeply and hold the pose for about 30 seconds to a minute. Feel release in the front of your left and outer right hips.

4. Gently come out of the pose, bring yourself back up to your hands and knees, and repeat on the opposite side.

5. **Modification:** If this pose feels too intense, place a folded blanket or a yoga block under your sitting bone on the bent knee side for support. It's okay if your chest can't touch the ground. Focus on relaxing your body and enjoying the stretch—the option to rest your head or chest on a pillow or yoga block.

High Pigeon

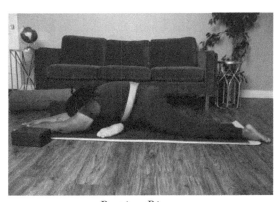

Resting Pigeon

As you move through these poses, focus on your breath and the sensations in your body, allowing any emotions that arise to come to the surface. This process helps you process and release these emotions, increasing emotional stability and resilience.

Incorporating somatic yoga into your daily life enhances emotional resilience and well-being. Start your day with a few gentle poses to set a positive tone.

1. For example, begin with a few rounds of **Cat-Cow** to wake up your spine, followed by **Child's Pose** to center yourself.

2. During the day, take short breaks to practice simple poses like **Forward Fold** or **Seated Spinal Twist**, which can help release tension and refocus your mind.

3. In the evening, unwind with restorative poses like **Legs-Up-The-Wall** or **Reclining Bound Angle Pose**, which promote relaxation and prepare the body for restful sleep.

Chapter 7: Pain Management Techniques

Imagine waking up every morning with a heavy weight on your neck and shoulders, a soreness that never disappears, no matter how much you stretch or massage. You're not alone. Many of us spend our days slumped over computers, hunched over our phones, or carrying heavy bags, leading to chronic neck and shoulder pain. These lifestyle and ergonomic factors contribute significantly to the discomfort we experience. Poor posture, for instance, causes your muscles to work overtime to support your head, leading to muscle fatigue and pain. Prolonged sitting exacerbates this by compressing the spine and tightening the muscles around your neck and shoulders.

7.1 Somatics for Chronic Neck and Shoulder Pain

Somatic exercises, which focus on mindful movement and body awareness, offer a solution. One effective exercise is the **neck roll**.

Try it Yourself: Neck Roll

1. Start by sitting comfortably with your back straight.

2. Slowly drop your chin to your chest, feeling the stretch along the back of your neck.

3. Inhale, gently roll your head towards your right shoulder, then tilt it back slightly.

4. Exhale and roll it towards your left shoulder before returning to the starting position. Repeat in the opposite direction.

5. The key here is to move slowly and mindfully, paying attention to your neck and shoulder sensations. This exercise helps stretch the muscles, improve flexibility, and release tension built up over time.

Neck Roll

Another beneficial movement is the "**shoulder shrug**."

Try it Yourself: Shoulder Shrug

1. Sit or stand with your arms relaxed by your sides.

2. Inhale deeply as you lift your shoulders towards your ears, squeezing them tightly. Hold for a few seconds, then exhale as you release your shoulders to their natural position.

3. Repeat this movement for about ten repetitions. The shoulder shrug targets the trapezius muscles, often tight and overworked in desk workers. Regularly practicing this exercise can alleviate tension and improve shoulder mobility.

Shoulder Shrug

Mindful awareness during these exercises enhances their effectiveness. As you perform each movement, focus on the sensations in your body. Notice any areas of tightness or discomfort and breathe into them, allowing the breath to help release the tension. This mindful approach helps manage and reduce pain and fosters a deeper connection with your body. By paying attention to how your body feels and moves, you can identify and address issues before they become chronic problems.

You can integrate these movements into your daily activities for those hectic days. For example, perform a quick shoulder shrug while waiting for a meeting or do a neck roll while on a call. These exercises are discreet and can be done almost anywhere, making them easy to incorporate into even the busiest schedules.

Try It Yourself: Daily Somatic Exercise for Neck and Shoulder Relief

1. **Neck Roll**:

   ○ Perform three slow, mindful neck rolls in each direction.

   ○ Focus on stretching and releasing tension.

2. **Shoulder Shrug**:

   ○ Complete ten repetitions, inhaling as you lift and exhaling as you release.

   ○ Pay attention to the sensations in your shoulders.

3. **Incorporate into Routine**:

   ○ Morning: Include in your stretch routine.

   ○ During Work: Take breaks every hour for quick exercises.

   ○ Evening: Wind down with a few repetitions before bed.

By making these somatic exercises a regular part of your routine, you can effectively manage and prevent chronic neck and shoulder pain. Remember, the key is consistency and mindfulness. Listen to your body, move gently, and breathe deeply.

7.2 Natural Relief for Arthritis through Gentle Movements

Arthritis is a condition that affects millions of adults, impacting the joints and causing symptoms like pain, swelling, stiffness, and reduced range of motion. The two most common types are osteoarthritis and rheumatoid arthritis. Osteoarthritis occurs when the protective cartilage cushions at the ends of your bones wear down over time, leading to pain and stiffness, especially in weight-bearing joints like the knees and hips. Rheumatoid arthritis, on the other hand, is an autoimmune disorder that primarily targets the lining of the joints, causing painful swelling that can eventually result in joint deformity. Both types of arthritis can significantly impact your quality of life, making everyday activities a challenge.

Somatic movements offer a gentle yet effective way to manage arthritis symptoms by improving joint fluidity and reducing stiffness. One beneficial exercise is the **seated hip opener**.

Try it Yourself: Seated Hip Opener

1. Sit comfortably on a chair with your feet flat on the ground. Place your right ankle on your left knee, forming a figure-four shape.

2. Gently press down on your right knee, feeling a stretch in your hip.

3. Hold for a few breaths, then switch sides. This movement helps to open the hips and alleviate stiffness, making it easier to move without pain.

4. **Modification**: if pressing down on your knee causes discomfort, hold the position without applying pressure.

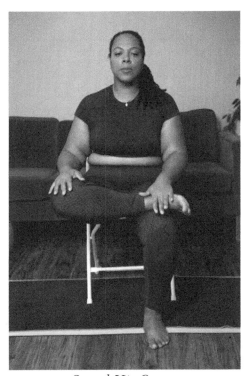

Seated Hip Opener

Another helpful exercise is the **wrist circles**.

Try it Yourself: Wrist Circles

1. Bend your elbows with your hands at shoulder height.

2. Slowly rotate your wrist in a circular motion, clockwise and counterclockwise. Repeat this movement several times on each side.

3. The key is to listen to your body and move within a pain-free range. Wrist circles are excellent for increasing flexibility and reducing stiffness in the wrist joints, which can be particularly beneficial for those with rheumatoid arthritis.

4. **Modification**: Extend one arm with the palm facing down. Use your other hand to support the extended arm just below the wrist. Begin with small, gentle rotations and increase the size of the circles as your comfort level improves.

Wrist Circles

Incorporating supportive practices can further enhance the benefits of somatic exercises for arthritis. Warm baths, for instance, can help to relax your muscles and reduce joint stiffness. Adding Epsom salts to your bathwater can provide additional relief, as the salts' magnesium helps reduce inflammation. After your bath, use a heating pad or warm compress to apply heat therapy to the affected joints. Heat therapy increases blood flow to the area, promoting healing and reducing pain.

Combining these practices with somatic movements creates a holistic approach to managing arthritis. For example, you might start your day with a warm bath to loosen your joints, followed by a few minutes of gentle wrist circles and seated hip openers. Take short breaks to perform these exercises throughout the day, especially if you've been sitting or standing for long periods. In the evening, apply heat therapy to sore joints to help them recover overnight. Imagine the relief of waking up with less stiffness, moving through your day with greater ease, and enjoying activities that arthritis once made difficult. These small but significant changes can lead to a marked improvement in your quality of life.

7.3 Somatic Solutions for Sciatica and Nerve Pain

Sciatica is a condition marked by pain that radiates along the path of the sciatic nerve, which branches from your lower back through your hips and down each leg. This pain can range from a mild ache to a burning sensation.

Simple activities like sitting, standing, or walking can make it unbearable. Common causes of sciatica include a herniated disk, bone spurs on the spine, or narrowing of the spine (spinal stenosis), which compresses part of the nerve. The resulting inflammation, pain, and often some numbness in the affected leg can significantly impact your quality of life.

Somatic exercises can be incredibly practical in addressing this. One targeted exercise is **hip dips.** This exercise is performed on all fours and involves lowering each hip towards the floor, alternating between hips.

Try it Yourself: Hip Dips

1. Start by positioning yourself on your hands and knees with your wrists directly under your shoulders and your knees under your hips.

2. Exhale and slowly lower your outer right hip to the floor. Keep your hands planted in front of you as you face your knees toward the left side of the room. Feel a slight twist in your spin while your hip lowers toward the ground.

3. Feel a deep stretch through your outer hip and lower back. Breathe and hold the position as long as you need to.

4. Inhale, lift your hip, and return to the center on your hands and knees.

5. Exhale, change sides, lower your left hip down and hold. Continue to alternate sides as many times as necessary to feel relief.

Hip Dips

This gentle movement helps to release tension in the lower back and hips, reducing pressure on the sciatic nerve. Move slowly and mindfully, paying attention to your lower back and hip sensations. Another effective exercise is the **figure-four stretch**.

Try it Yourself: Figure Four Stretch

1. Lie on your back with your knees bent and feet flat on the floor.

2. Cross your right ankle over your left knee, forming a figure-four shape.

3. Gently pull your left thigh towards your chest, feeling a stretch in your right hip and glute. Hold for several breaths, then switch sides. This stretch helps to open the hips and relieve pressure on the sciatic nerve, providing significant relief from pain.

Figure Four Starting Position

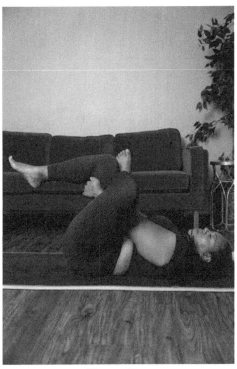

Figure Four

Try hip lifts to target the hip flexor and lower back for relief.

Try it Yourself: Hip Lifts

1. Sit on the floor in a "Stag" position, with the bottom of your right foot touching the top of your left thigh and your left foot behind you.

2. Inhale, twist your chest to the right, and bring your hands to the outside of your right hip.

3. Lift your left hip as you twist to the right. Feel the stretch through your left hip flexor. To deepen the twist, use your right knee and thigh for leverage.

4. Inhale and exhale as you lift and lower your left hip to release tension and find mobility in the hip flexor.

5. Exhale and release back to center. Switch sides and change directions with your left foot touching the top of your right thigh and your right foot behind you.

6. Inhale, twist to the left and lift your right hip. Exhale back to center. Do this as many times as necessary.

Hip Lifts

In addition to these exercises, reducing inflammation can further alleviate nerve pain. Incorporating anti-in-flammatory foods into your diet, such as leafy greens and fatty fish like salmon and nuts, can make a noticeable difference. Turmeric, known for its anti-inflammatory properties, can be added to meals or taken as a supplement. Staying hydrated is also crucial, as dehydration can contribute to muscle stiffness and inflammation. Regular hydration helps to keep your muscles and tissues supple, reducing the likelihood of flare-ups.

Lifestyle changes can also complement somatic practices. Maintaining a healthy weight reduces the stress on your spine, which can help prevent sciatic pain. Regular physical activity, such as walking or swimming, promotes overall spinal health and reduces inflammation. Avoid prolonged sitting by taking breaks to stand, stretch, or walk every 30 minutes. If you work at a desk, consider an ergonomic chair that supports your lower back and encourages good posture.

Developing a sustainable routine of somatic exercises is essential for managing and preventing sciatica symptoms. Start with a daily practice, dedicating 10-15 minutes each morning or evening to exercises like the pelvic clock and figure-four stretch. Gradually increase the duration and variety of your exercises as you become more comfortable. Consistency is key, so find a routine that fits into your daily life and stick with it. Keep track of your progress in a journal, noting any changes in your pain levels or mobility to help you identify which exercises are most effective for you and make any necessary adjustments to your routine.

Integrating these somatic exercises with dietary and lifestyle changes can create a holistic approach to managing sciatica and nerve pain. The goal is to temporarily relieve pain, improve overall spinal health, and prevent future flare-ups. Imagine the relief of moving through your day without the nagging pain, feeling more flexible and at ease with every step you take.

7.4 Preventing Headaches & Migraines with Routine Somatic Practices

Headaches can be a real pain, both literally and figuratively. They come in various forms, each with its own set of triggers. Tension headaches are the most common, often caused by muscle strain in the neck and shoulders due to poor posture, stress, or prolonged screen time. Conversely, migraines are more severe and often triggered by hormonal changes, certain foods, or environmental stimuli such as bright lights or loud noises. Understanding the type of headache you're dealing with can help you choose the most effective somatic exercises for relief.

The **neck roll** is one of the most effective somatic headache management techniques. This exercise targets the tension in your neck and shoulders that often contributes to headaches.

Try it Yourself: Neck Roll

1. Start by sitting comfortably with your back straight.

2. Slowly drop your chin to your chest, feeling the stretch along the back of your neck.

3. Inhale, gently roll your head towards your right shoulder, and tilt it back slightly.

4. Exhale and roll it towards your left shoulder before returning to the starting position. Repeat in the opposite direction.

5. The key here is to move slowly and mindfully, paying attention to your neck and shoulder sensations. This exercise helps stretch the muscles, improve flexibility, and release tension built up over time.

Neck Roll Position 1

Neck Roll

Another helpful technique is the **shoulder shrug**.

Try it Yourself: Shoulder Shrug

1. Inhale intensely, lift your shoulders toward your ears, hold for a few seconds, and then exhale as you release your shoulders back down. You can do these exercises anytime you feel a headache, and they provide immediate relief.

2. Incorporating specific somatic exercises into your routine can significantly reduce the frequency and intensity of migraines. One effective exercise is the **scapular release**.

Try it Yourself: Scapular Release

1. Sit comfortably with your back straight.

2. Slowly roll your shoulders forward in a circular motion, then reverse the direction. This movement helps release tension in the upper back and shoulders, areas often affected by migraines.

Scapular Release

Another helpful exercise is the **gentle neck stretch**.

Try it Yourself: Gentle Neck Stretch

1. Sit or stand with your arms at your sides.

2. Tilt your head towards one shoulder, using your hand to deepen the stretch gently.

3. Hold for a few breaths, then switch sides. This stretch helps to alleviate tension in the neck, which can contribute to migraine pain.

Neck Stretch

Try It Yourself: Daily Somatic Exercise Checklist

1. **Neck Roll:**

    a. Perform three slow, mindful neck rolls in each direction.

    b. Focus on stretching and releasing tension.

2. **Shoulder Shrug**:

    a. Complete ten repetitions, inhaling as you lift and exhaling as you release.

    b. Pay attention to the sensations in your shoulders.

3. **Scapular Release**:

    a. Complete five forward shoulder circles and five reverse, inhaling as you lift and exhaling as you release.

    b. Pay attention to the sensations in your shoulders.

4. **Gentle Neck Stretch**:

    a. Complete five head tilts to the left and five to the right, inhaling as you lift and exhaling as you release.

    b. Pay attention to the sensations in your shoulders.

5. **Incorporate into Routine**:

    a. Morning: Include in your stretch routine.

    b. During Work: Take breaks every hour for quick exercises.

    c. Evening: Wind down with a few repetitions before bed.

Environmental and lifestyle adjustments can also play a crucial role in managing headaches. Ensure you stay hydrated throughout the day, as dehydration is a common headache trigger. Adjust the lighting in your workspace to reduce glare and eye strain, and consider using a humidifier if the air is dry. Sleep posture is equally essential; invest in a supportive pillow to align your neck with your spine. Avoid sleeping on your stomach, as this can strain your neck. By making these small changes, you can complement your somatic practices and create a holistic approach to headache management.

Mindfulness and stress reduction techniques complement these somatic exercises, enhancing their effectiveness. Practicing mindfulness involves focusing on the present moment without judgment. A straightforward method is the **body scan**.

1. Find a quiet place to sit or lie down comfortably. Close your eyes and take a few deep breaths.

2. Slowly bring your attention to different body parts, starting from your toes and moving up to your head.

3. Notice any areas of tension or discomfort and breathe into them, allowing the tension to release with each exhale.

4. This practice helps manage stress and increases your awareness of early migraine symptoms, allowing for timely intervention.

Lifestyle adjustments also play a significant role in managing and preventing migraines. Adequate sleep is crucial; aim for 7-9 hours of quality sleep each night. Establish a regular sleep schedule by going to bed and waking up at the same time every day, even on weekends. Hydration is another crucial factor. Dehydration can trigger migraines, so drink plenty of water throughout the day. Limit your intake of caffeine and alcohol, as both can contribute to dehydration and trigger migraines.

Additionally, pay attention to your diet. Certain foods, such as aged cheeses, processed meats, and foods containing MSG, can trigger migraines in some people. Keeping a food diary can help you identify and avoid these triggers.

Regular physical activity is also beneficial. Aim for at least 30 minutes of moderate exercise most days of the week. Walking, swimming, or yoga can help reduce stress and improve overall health, making migraines less frequent and severe. Finally, consider creating a migraine-friendly environment. Reduce exposure to bright lights and loud noises, and use blackout curtains in your bedroom to create a dark, quiet space for sleep. Aromatherapy can also help; essential oils like lavender and peppermint may alleviate migraine symptoms for some people.

Creating a daily preventive routine can significantly reduce the frequency and intensity of headaches.

Try It Yourself: Daily Somatic Exercises Routine for Headaches

1. Start your day with a few minutes of **neck rolls and shoulder shrugs** to loosen up your muscles.

2. Take short breaks throughout the day to stretch and relax your neck and shoulders. Incorporate **gentle jaw exercises,** too, as clenching can contribute to tension headaches.

3. Before bed, practice **body scans** and **deep breathing exercises** to calm your nervous system and prepare your body for restful sleep.

Integrating these somatic exercises, mindfulness practices, and lifestyle adjustments into your daily routine can create a comprehensive approach to migraine prevention. The goal is to reduce the frequency and intensity of migraines and improve your overall quality of life. Imagine the relief of fewer migraine days, the ability to enjoy activities without the looming threat of pain, and the empowerment that comes from managing your health proactively. This holistic approach offers a pathway to a more balanced and fulfilling life, free from the constant burden of migraines.

Chapter 8: Building a Somatic Lifestyle

Imagine sipping your morning coffee, savoring that first quiet moment of the day. As you stand by the kitchen counter, you feel a familiar tightness in your lower back and shoulders. You could ignore it and hope it fades on its own or use this moment to integrate a somatic practice that has the power to transform your day from the start. This chapter is about weaving somatic exercises seamlessly into your daily routine, turning ordinary moments into opportunities for profound well-being.

8.1 Integrating Somatics into Your Daily Routine

Integrating small somatic practices into your day is simpler than you think. It's not about finding extra time but about making the most of the moments you already have. For instance, while brushing your teeth, you can stand with your feet hip-width apart and gently shift your weight from one foot to the other. This simple movement helps you become more aware of your body's balance and alignment. Or consider the time spent waiting for your morning coffee to brew—you can use this moment to perform gentle neck rolls, easing the tension built up from a night of sleep.

Cue-based habits are another powerful way to ensure consistent somatic practice. Think about the natural cues in your environment that can prompt you to engage in short exercises. For example, whenever you sit at your desk, take a moment to do a **seated spinal twist**.

Try it Yourself: Seated Spinal Twist

1. Place your right hand on the back of your chair and your left hand on your right knee.

2. Inhale deeply and exhale as you gently twist your torso to the right. This will help relieve any tension in your spine and serve as a mental reset before you dive into work.

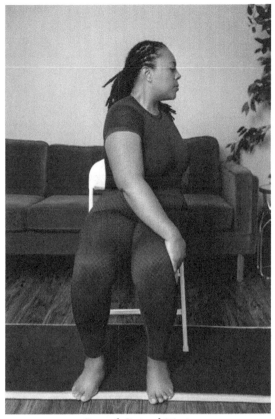

Seated Spinal Twist

Linking somatic exercises to daily activities transforms mundane tasks into mindfulness and body awareness moments. When cooking dinner, for instance, you can practice **gentle calf raises**.

Try it Yourself: Gentle Calf Raises

1. Stand with your feet parallel, rise onto your toes as you inhale, and lower your heels as you exhale.

2. This subtle movement strengthens your calves and improves circulation.

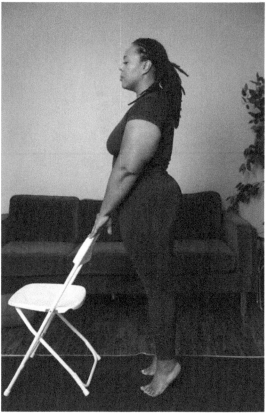

Calf Raises

Similarly, try a few **forward folds** while folding laundry to stretch your hamstrings and release lower back tension. Associating these movements with regular activities builds a natural and sustainable routine.

Creating rituals that anchor your day is a powerful way to integrate somatics into your lifestyle. Begin your morning with a simple body scan. Before getting out of bed, take a few deep breaths and mentally scan your body from head to toe. Notice any areas of tension and consciously release them with each exhale. This sets a positive tone for your day, grounding you in your body and breath. Establish a wind-down sequence in the evening to signal your body that it's time to relax and prepare for sleep. A few minutes of gentle stretches and deep breathing can help release the day's accumulated stress and promote restful sleep.

Try It Yourself: Somatic Integration Checklist

1. **Morning Routine:**

    ○ **Body Scan:** Before getting out of bed, take deep breaths and mentally scan your body from head to toe.

    ○ **Neck Rolls:** While waiting for your coffee, gently roll your neck to release tension.

2. **Throughout the Day:**

    ○ **Seated Spinal Twist:** Use your desk chair as a cue to perform a seated spinal twist.

- **Calf Raises:** While cooking, rise onto your toes and lower back down with each breath.

3. **Evening Ritual:**

- **Forward Folds:** Incorporate gentle forward folds while folding laundry to stretch your hamstrings.

- **Wind-Down Sequence:** End your day with a few minutes of gentle stretches and deep breathing.

Integrating these somatic practices into your daily routine creates a lifestyle that supports continuous well-being without feeling like an additional chore. These small, mindful movements can profoundly impact your physical and mental health, transforming everyday moments into opportunities for self-care and mindfulness.

8.2 Creating a Personalized Somatic Exercise Plan

Creating a personalized somatic exercise plan is not a one-size-fits-all approach. It begins with a thoughtful assessment of your personal health needs and limitations. Start by reflecting on your current physical condition. Are there specific areas where you experience chronic pain or stiffness? Are any injuries or medical conditions affecting your ability to perform specific movements? Take note of these factors, as they will guide the customization of your exercise plan, ensuring it's tailored to your unique needs.

Additionally, consider your lifestyle and daily activities. If you have a sedentary job, your plan might focus on exercises that counteract the effects of prolonged sitting. On the other hand, if you're already physically active, your plan might include exercises that enhance flexibility and relaxation.

Setting realistic and achievable goals is crucial for maintaining motivation and tracking progress in your somatic exercise plan. Begin by identifying what you hope to achieve with somatic exercises. Are you seeking to reduce stress, alleviate chronic pain, or improve mobility? Once you clearly understand your goals, break them down into smaller, manageable steps. For example, if your goal is to reduce lower back pain, start with simple exercises like pelvic tilts and gradually progress to more advanced movements as your comfort level increases. Setting specific, measurable goals helps you stay focused and allows you to celebrate your progress along the way.

Structuring your personalized plan involves determining exercise frequency, duration, and progression. Start with a realistic schedule that fits into your daily routine. It's better to commit to a few minutes of practice each day than to set an ambitious goal that you can't sustain. Begin with shorter sessions, such as five to ten minutes, and gradually increase the duration as you become more comfortable with the exercises, rotating through various types of movement. Over time, as you build strength and flexibility, you can introduce more challenging exercises to keep your practice engaging and effective.

Tracking your progress is essential to maintaining a personalized somatic exercise plan. Keep a journal or log where you record your daily practice, noting which exercises you performed and any observations about how your body felt. This practice helps you stay accountable and allows you to identify patterns and adjust as needed. If you notice that specific exercises consistently alleviate pain or improve your mood, you can prioritize them in your routine. Conversely, if an exercise causes discomfort, you may need to modify or replace it with a different movement. Tracking your progress also provides a sense of accomplishment, reinforcing your commitment to the practice.

Try It Yourself: Goal Setting Worksheet

1. **Identify Your Primary Goal**: What do you hope to achieve with somatic exercises (e.g., reduce stress, improve flexibility)?

2. **Break It Down**: List smaller, specific steps to help you reach your primary goal.

3. **Set a Timeline**: Determine a realistic timeframe for achieving each step.

4. **Track Your Progress**: Use a journal or log to record your daily practice and any observations about your body.

By assessing your needs, setting realistic goals, structuring your plan, and tracking your progress, you can create a somatic exercise plan tailored to your unique requirements. This personalized approach ensures that your practice is practical and sustainable, helping you achieve your health and wellness goals.

8.3 Somatic Exercises for Spiritual Development

Imagine standing in a quiet room, sunlight streaming through the window, casting a warm glow on the floor. You begin to move slowly, mindfully, feeling each muscle stretch and contract. This isn't just exercise—it's a form of moving meditation that enhances your spiritual mindfulness and presence. Somatic exercises can be a powerful tool for spiritual development, helping you cultivate a deeper connection with yourself and the world around you.

Mindfulness and meditation are cornerstones of spiritual practice, and somatic exercises naturally complement these practices. As you move, focus on each breath and sensation, turning your awareness inward. This mindful movement becomes a form of meditation, allowing you to stay present and fully experience your body. For example, as you perform a slow spinal twist, focus on the breath entering and leaving your lungs and the gentle stretch of your spine. This practice enhances your physical flexibility and deepens your spiritual awareness and grounding.

These exercises encourage introspection and self-awareness, fostering a stronger sense of self. You become more attuned to your body's signals and emotions when you engage in somatic movements. This heightened awareness can lead to personal insights and a better understanding of your own needs and desires. For instance, during a gentle forward fold, you might notice tension in your lower back and realize it's linked to stress or unresolved emotions. Acknowledging and addressing these feelings fosters emotional and spiritual growth.

Integrating philosophical and spiritual concepts into your somatic practice can further enhance your experience. Consider incorporating the principles of acceptance and letting go into your routine. As you move through each exercise, practice accepting your body as it is without judgment. Let go of any tension or negative thoughts, focusing instead on the present moment. This approach improves your physical well-being and nurtures a more compassionate and positive mindset. You could, for instance, dedicate a session to exploring the concept of balance—not just physical balance but emotional and spiritual equilibrium as well.

Some specific somatic exercises are particularly effective for enhancing spiritual development. Grounding techniques can help you feel more centered and connected to your surroundings. Try standing firmly planted on the ground and visualizing roots growing from your soles into the earth. Centering exercises, like the pelvic tilt, can bring your focus to your core, fostering a sense of stability and inner strength. As you perform these movements, imagine drawing energy from the earth, filling your body with vitality and peace.

Reflection Section: Spiritual Connection Through Somatics

Grounding Technique:

1. **Exercise:** Stand with feet hip-width apart and visualize roots growing from your feet into the ground.

2. **Focus:** Feel the connection with the earth, drawing energy upward.

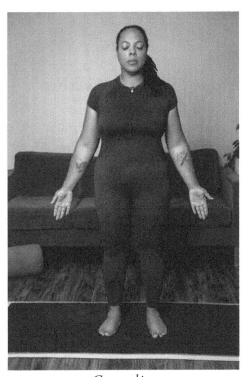

Grounding

Centering Technique:

1. **Exercise:** Perform a pelvic tilt, focusing on your core.

2. **Focus:** Imagine drawing strength and stability from your center.

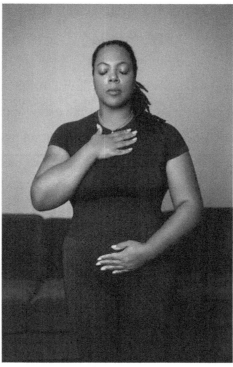

Centering

By incorporating these practices into your daily routine, you can create a somatic experience that enhances your physical health and nourishes your spiritual well-being.

8.4 Creating a Community Around Somatic Practices

Imagine the comfort of knowing that you're not alone in your quest for better health. Practicing somatic exercises within a community offers numerous benefits, including mutual support, shared learning, and enhanced motivation. When you're part of a group, you have people to share your progress with, seek advice from, and celebrate milestones together. The shared experiences create a sense of belonging and accountability, making staying committed to your practice more accessible. You'll find that learning from others' experiences can provide new insights and techniques you might not have discovered.

Starting a local somatic exercise group can be a rewarding endeavor. Begin by reaching out to friends, family, or coworkers who might be interested in joining you. Use social media platforms or community bulletin boards to spread the word. Find a suitable location for your meetings—this could be a local park, community center, or even someone's living room. Once you have a group and a location, set a regular meeting schedule that works for everyone. Keep the sessions informal and welcoming, encouraging members to share their experiences and goals. You might consider rotating leadership roles so that everyone has a chance to guide the group and contribute their unique perspectives.

Online communities offer another avenue for engaging with others who share your interest in somatic practices. Join forums, social media groups, or virtual classes dedicated to somatic exercises. Platforms like Facebook, Reddit, and specialized online forums provide spaces where you can ask questions, share tips, and connect with practitioners worldwide. Virtual classes and webinars are also valuable resources, offering professional guidance and the opportunity to practice with others in real-time, even if you're physically apart. Engaging with these online communities can provide a broader perspective and introduce you to diverse techniques and philosophies.

Organizing events and workshops is a fantastic way to foster a sense of belonging and collective growth within your somatic community. Start by planning small events like themed practice sessions or guest speaker presentations. Workshops can be more in-depth, focusing on specific aspects of somatic exercises, such as breathwork or stress management. Invite local experts or experienced practitioners to lead these sessions, providing attendees with valuable knowledge and new skills. Promote these events through your community group, social media, and local bulletin boards to attract participants. These gatherings enhance individual practices and strengthen the community as a whole, creating a supportive network that motivates and inspires everyone involved.

Interactive Element: Community Building Checklist

1. **Identify Interested Members:**

   o Use social media to reach out to friends, family, and coworkers.

2. **Choose a Location:**

   o Local park, community center, or someone's living room.

3. **Set a Schedule:**

   o Regular meetings that suit everyone's availability.

4. **Promote Events:**

   o Use social media, community boards, and word-of-mouth.

5. **Plan Workshops:**

   o Focus on specific somatic aspects, invite experts, and share knowledge.

We invite you to join our Somatice Exercise Made Simple Facebook Group. Creating a somatic community enriches your practice and fosters a sense of connection and support. These shared experiences and collective efforts can significantly enhance your journey toward better health and well-being, making the process more enjoyable and sustainable for everyone involved.

Join Our Somatic Exercise Facebook Community

8.5 Celebrating Progress: Recognizing and Sustaining Success in Your Somatic Journey

One of the most rewarding aspects of integrating somatic exercises into your life is witnessing your progress. Tracking and reflecting on your journey can be incredibly motivating. Keeping a journal or log of your experiences and growth helps you see how far you've come. Note down the exercises you practice, any physical changes you observe, and how you feel emotionally and mentally. This provides a record of your development and helps identify patterns and areas that may need more focus. Journaling can be as simple as jotting down a few sentences each day about your practice and any noticeable changes, or it can be more detailed, including reflections on your emotional state and any insights gained during your exercises.

Setting milestones and celebrating achievements—no matter how small—can keep you motivated and committed. Break down your larger goals into smaller, manageable milestones. For example, suppose your goal is to reduce chronic back pain. In that case, a milestone might be performing a specific exercise without discomfort. Celebrate these achievements in a way that feels meaningful to you. This could be treating yourself to a relaxing bath, sharing your success with a friend, or simply taking a moment to acknowledge your hard work and dedication. These celebrations are positive reinforcement, encouraging you to continue your practice enthusiastically.

Long-term commitment to somatic practices requires strategies that adapt as you evolve. Continuous learning is key. As you become more comfortable with basic exercises, seek out new techniques to keep your practice engaging. Attend workshops, read articles, or watch instructional videos to expand your knowledge. Adapt your practice to fit your changing needs and lifestyle. For instance, if you start a new job with a longer commute, find ways to incorporate somatic exercises during breaks or while traveling. Flexibility in your approach ensures that somatic practices remain a consistent part of your life, providing ongoing benefits.

Sharing your stories and successes can inspire others and foster a sense of community. Talk about your experiences with friends, family, or online groups dedicated to somatic practices. Sharing provides you with a sense of accomplishment and encourages others to embark on their own somatic journeys. Your story might motivate someone else to start practicing, creating a ripple effect extending somatic exercises' benefits to a broader audience. Additionally, hearing others' successes can reignite your own motivation, reminding you of the collective power of shared experiences.

Reflection Section: Celebrating Your Progress

1. **Track Your Journey:**

   ◦ Keep a journal noting exercises, physical changes, and emotional states.

2. **Set and Celebrate Milestones:**

   ◦ Break down goals into smaller milestones and celebrate achievements.

3. **Commit to Continuous Learning:**

   ◦ Seek out new techniques and adapt your practice to fit your evolving needs.

4. **Share Your Success:**

   ◦ Inspire others by sharing your experiences and hearing their stories.

Recognizing and celebrating your progress in somatic practices reinforces your commitment and enhances your overall well-being. Tracking your journey, setting milestones, and sharing your successes create a supportive framework that keeps you motivated and engaged. This reflective practice ensures that somatic exercises remain a meaningful and rewarding part of your life, contributing to your long-term health and happiness.

As we move forward, we'll explore additional ways to deepen your practice and integrate these principles into your everyday life.

Conclusion

As we end our journey together in "Somatic Exercise Made Simple," let's take a moment to reflect on the incredible path you've embarked upon. From the initial discovery of somatic exercises to the deep exploration of mind-body harmony, you've learned how to integrate these gentle yet powerful practices into your daily life. This journey has not just been about learning new movements; it's been about experiencing a transformation in your physical, mental, and emotional well-being.

Throughout the chapters, you've discovered the importance of body awareness—how tuning into your internal perceptions can play a crucial role in healing and sustaining health. You've also seen how accessible somatic exercises are, suitable for people of all ages and abilities. Whether you're dealing with chronic pain, stress, or simply seeking a more balanced life, these exercises provide a pathway to enhanced well-being.

The holistic approach to health that somatic exercises offer is truly remarkable. By addressing not just the physical aspects but also mental, emotional, and even spiritual well-being, you've laid the foundation for a balanced and harmonious life. Remember, it's not just about the movements; it's about the mindfulness, the connection to your inner self, and the peace that comes from within.

As you stand at the threshold of making somatic practices a lifelong habit, I urge you to continue this exploration with enthusiasm and curiosity. These exercises are more than just a routine—they are a journey toward self-awareness, health, and harmony. Keep experimenting, keep listening to your body, and keep growing. Your journey is unique, and your somatic practice should reflect your needs, goals, and circumstances.

Incorporating somatic principles and exercises into your daily life can be a game-changer. Start small—maybe a few minutes in the morning and a few more in the evening. Use the cues and habits we've discussed to integrate these practices into your routine seamlessly. Over time, these small changes will accumulate, creating a personalized somatic lifestyle that supports your holistic health.

I'd also love for you to share your experiences and successes with others. Whether through social media, community groups, or personal conversations, your journey can inspire and support those around you. Building a community around somatic exercises enriches your practice and creates a network of encouragement and shared growth.

Remember, you have the power to create change, heal, and find balance. Somatic exercises are tools to help you unlock this potential. Each movement, breath, and moment of mindfulness brings you closer to a state of harmony and well-being.

Acknowledge your effort, time, and commitment in exploring somatic exercises through this book. Your progress, no matter how small it may seem, is a testament to your dedication and willingness to improve your life. Celebrate these achievements and look forward to the continued journey with confidence and curiosity.

Finally, I am grateful for joining me on this journey. I hope "Somatic Exercise Made Simple" has provided you with valuable insights, practical tools, and the inspiration needed to pursue a holistic health and mind-body harmony path. Thank you for allowing me to join your journey towards a healthier, more balanced life. **If you enjoyed the material and found it valuable and helpful, please leave a review on Amazon.**

With warmth and appreciation,

Dr. Danielle Griffin

Printable 28-Day Tracking Guide

Now, you have everything you need to develop a personalized 28-day plan for lasting health improvements. Throughout the book, we provided you with numerous Somatic Exercise Sequences to target various parts of the body and various needs and conditions. Feel free to jump to the sections you need the most and use the guide to plan your next 4 weeks of activity. We know that you are a busy, health-conscious adult seeking Mind-Body Harmony, and preparing your Somatic Exercises should be Simple! You can pair multiple sequences to target multiple things at a time or work on one area of the body each week. The choice is yours.

The links below give you access to printable versions of the guide, which you can use to continue your practice. Having a printable version allows for flexibility and changes.

Scan the QR code below or click the link to Download printable versions of the Weekly Exercise Tracking Worksheets.

https://drive.google.com/file/d/1d5Uzy95lqijNLK3YyRldnI3ylinxsVTo/view?usp=sharing

Printable 28-Day Tracking Guide

WEEKLY TRACKING

Document Your Weekly Progress

Training Date	Exercises	Meditation Time	Breath Work Exercises	How do you feel?

Start Date: _____

Areas of Focus or Concern: _____

References

A Brief History of Somatic Education https://essentialsomatics.com/a-brief-history-of-somatic-education/

Top-Down and Bottom-Up Mechanisms in Mind-Body ... https://www.ncbi.nlm.nih.gov/pmc/articles/PMC2818254/

Somatic Therapy: Benefits, Types And Efficacy https://www.forbes.com/health/mind/somatic-therapy/

Somatic experiencing – effectiveness and key factors of a ... https://www.ncbi.nlm.nih.gov/pmc/articles/PMC8276649/

6 Steps to Create Your Own Meditation Space https://www.beachbodyondemand.com/blog/meditation-space

Warm-up and cool-down activities https://www.nhsinform.scot/healthy-living/keeping-active/warm-up-and-cool-down-activities/

Somatic Stretching: How It Works, Benefits, and Starter ... https://www.everydayhealth.com/fitness/what-is-somatic-stretching/

Clinical Somatics Testimonials https://somaticmovementcenter.com/somatics-testimonials/

Moving With Pain: What Principles From Somatic Practices ... https://www.ncbi.nlm.nih.gov/pmc/articles/PMC7868595/

Workout Schedules: Weekly Samples for Each Fitness Level https://www.verywellfit.com/sample-workout-schedule-1230758

The Best Mind Body Connection Exercises [From A Therapist] https://www.robyngraycounseling.com/blog/mind-body-exercises

Modifying Exercises and Adjusting Your Student https://somaticmovementcenter.com/wp-content/uploads/2020/09/Modifying-and-Adjusting-1.pdf

Understanding the stress response https://www.health.harvard.edu/staying-healthy/understanding-the-stress-response

Breathing Techniques for Stress Relief https://www.webmd.com/balance/stress-management/stress-relief-breathing-techniques

Benefits of Progressive Muscle Relaxation (PMR) https://www.verywellhealth.com/progressive-muscle-relaxation-5225381

12 Effective Somatic Therapy Exercises for Holistic Healing https://www.monakirstein.com/somatic-therapy-exercises/

Moving With Pain: What Principles From Somatic Practices ... https://www.ncbi.nlm.nih.gov/pmc/articles/PMC7868595/

6 Ways Somatic Movement Can Benefit Your Mind and Body https://www.onepeloton.com/blog/somatic-movement/

Clinical Somatics Testimonials https://somaticmovementcenter.com/somatics-testimonials/

12 Effective Somatic Therapy Exercises for Holistic Healing https://www.monakirstein.com/somatic-therapy-exercises/

Improving your mobility - Harvard Health https://www.health.harvard.edu/exercise-and-fitness/improving-your-mobility

Stretching: Focus on flexibility https://www.mayoclinic.org/healthy-lifestyle/fitness/in-depth/stretching/art-20047931

5 Joint Mobility Exercises to Improve Flexibility and Function https://www.healthline.com/health/fitness-exercise/joint-mobility-exercises

Clinical Somatics Testimonials https://somaticmovementcenter.com/somatics-testimonials/

Relaxation techniques: Try these steps to lower stress https://www.mayoclinic.org/healthy-lifestyle/stress-management/in-depth/relaxation-technique/art-20045368

Getting Started with Mindful Movement https://www.mindful.org/getting-started-with-mindful-movement/

Guided Imagery Scripts: Free Relaxation Scripts https://www.innerhealthstudio.com/guided-imagery-scripts.html

How to Make Mindfulness Part of Your Daily Routine https://info.totalwellnesshealth.com/blog/how-to-make-mindfulness-part-of-your-daily-routine

Benefits of Somatic Exercises https://www.runnersworld.com/health-injuries/a46096070/guide-to-somatic-exercises/

5 Ways To Stimulate Your Vagus Nerve https://health.clevelandclinic.org/vagus-nerve-stimulation

Somatic Movement: What It Is, Benefits, and Tips - Peloton https://www.onepeloton.co.uk/blog/somatic-movement/#:~:text=%E2%80%9CSomatic%20movement%20helps%20people%20get,the%20outcome%2C%E2%80%9D%20she%20says.

Somatic Exercises: Stress Relief for Aching Bodies https://www.wellandgood.com/somatic-exercises/

Effect of breathwork on stress and mental health: A meta- ... https://www.nature.com/articles/s41598-022-27247-y

Diaphragmatic Breathing Exercises & Benefits https://my.clevelandclinic.org/health/articles/9445-diaphragmatic-breathing

How and Why to Perform Bhastrika Breath https://chopra.com/blogs/yoga/how-and-why-to-perform-bhastrika-breath

Somatic Breathwork: The Healing Power of an Ancient Practice https://www.ryandelaney.co/blog/somatic-breathwork

Well-being Assessments https://hfh.fas.harvard.edu/shorter-and-longer-well-being-assessments

Make Your Exercise Goals SMART! | Illinois Extension | UIUC https://eat-move-save.extension.illinois.edu/blog/make-your-exercise-goals-smart

How to Exercise With Chronic Pain https://www.nytimes.com/2021/11/09/well/move/exercise-chronic-pain.html

Clinical Somatics Testimonials https://somaticmovementcenter.com/somatics-testimonials/

Getting Started: Tips for Long-term Exercise Success https://www.heart.org/en/healthy-living/fitness/getting-active/getting-started---tips-for-long-term-exercise-success

Social reward and support effects on exercise experiences ... https://www.ncbi.nlm.nih.gov/pmc/articles/PMC8443045/

Creating An Awesome Home Workout Environment https://central.gymshark.com/article/exercise-at-home-creating-an-awesome-home-workout-environment

Clinical Somatics Testimonials https://somaticmovementcenter.com/somatics-testimonials/

Made in the USA
Las Vegas, NV
23 December 2024

15289363R00077